# SAN G D YUNGUE

## AS SEEN BY AN ARCHAEOLOGIST

*FLORENCE HAWLEY ELLIS*

Sunstone Press
*Santa Fe, New Mexico*
in conjunction with
The Florence Hawley Ellis
Museum of Anthropology
at
Ghost Ranch
Abiquiu, New Mexico
87510

Dedicated to
a Great Man
who made our publications possible
Jim Hall
There is no other like him

Library of Congress Cataloging in Publication Data:

Ellis, Florence Hawley
    San Gabriel del Yungue as seen by an archaeologist / by Florence Hawley Ellis.
        p.    cm.
    Bibliography: p.
 '  Includes index.
    ISBN: 0-86534-129-X : $10.95
    1. Yungue Site (N.M.)  2. Pueblo Indians--Antiquities.  3. San Gabriel del Yungue
(N.M.)--ANtiquities.  4. New Mexico--Antiquities.  5. Indians of North America--New
Mexico--Antiquities. I. Florence Hawley Ellis Museum of Anthropology. II. Title.
E99.P9E43    1989
978.9'52--dc19                                                          89-4212
                                                                       CIP

Published in 1989 by SUNSTONE PRESS
                Post Office Box 2321
                Santa Fe, NM 87504-2321 / USA


in conjunction with The Florence Hawley Ellis
Museum of Anthropology at
Ghost Ranch, Abiquiu, New Mexico 87510

# Table of Contents

# List of Illustrations

# Preface

It was in 1959 that I received a letter from the Governor of San Juan Pueblo requesting that we bring that summer's archaeological field school to excavate a long unused portion of San Juan Pueblo. According to traditions of that tribe, all or some of the southwestern end of this part of San Juan, on the west bank of the Rio Grande, had been remodeled by Oñate's Spanish soldier-settlers so that the they would feel more at home using that section as living quarters than using native style architecture.

Considering the difficulties of obtaining native permission for archaeologists to work on their land, we could not overlook this overture despite previous plans for that summer's work. Hence mid-June found us mapping, measuring, and excavating where the position of houses, irrigation ditches, roads, and other features did not make it impossible. Two more six week summer sessions in the succeeding two years produced most of what still could be traced, including the first permanent church, tentatively the oldest in the United States, for which searches had been going on over a period of many years before we were invited to work upon this important site.

But at the end of our three conceded seasons, there were no immediate funds into which we could dip for publication. By this time, our students were living in some of Ghost Ranch's summer quarters. Our evening study sessions at the Ranch were open to all interested, and the details of our discoveries were happily taken in by daytime visitors. There no longer was a question as to whether the portion of San Juan Pueblo which we were asked to investigate by excavation was, indeed, the section redesigned for their own use by Oñate, his friars, and his soldier-settlers.

Later, Jim Hall, director of Ghost Ranch, saw a need which the Ranch could aid by starting a fund, begun with donations from archaeology students and friends, and continued with donations from friends of the museum, as a birthday present on the 80th and later birthdays of Dr. Florence Ellis, to be used as an endowment for the Florence Hawley Ellis Museum at Ghost Ranch, where the best of the Yungue finds have been on exhibit for many years. The first use of this fund was to initiate the publication program for research in progress. The series of papers, backed by these funds, began with one which covered the first archaeological excavation and study handled under the auspices of that museum. This is our second report, with more planned for the next few years.

5

And so, with deep gratitude to Jim, our always friend, aid, and inspiration, we shall pursue the study of man and his works in the past, with hope that such will enhance man's further understanding of our future. We also want to thank the careful work of our excavators; the accurate reports of the crew chiefs; Ghost Ranch which housed the excavators and has backed us all along; the Pueblo Governor who requested our excavation of the Yungue mounds; the various Indians who through their intuitive knowledge provided their special finds to us and the Museums for study; the various researchers who have helped analyze the artifacts and the data from this site; the publication crew who have typed, edited, and repeated those jobs again and again to ready the manuscript for printing; Lou Baker who has so kindly provided production of the camera ready manuscript; Andrea my daughter/assistant who typed, edited and has seen to the orchestration of the many details of publication; the publication house itself; and most of all Jim Hall without whom you would not have been reading this book.

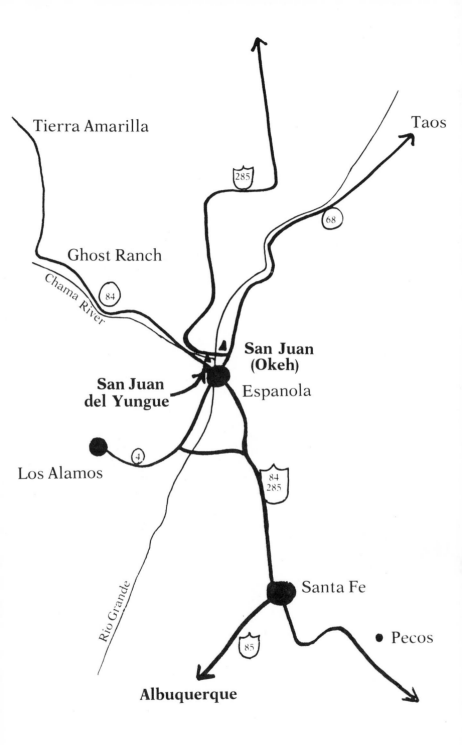

Tierra Amarilla

Taos

Ghost Ranch

Chama River

84

San Juan
(Okeh)

San Juan
del Yungue

Espanola

Los Alamos

4

84
285

Rio Grande

Santa Fe

Pecos

85

Albuquerque

285

68

Andrea Dodge 1988

7

*Brass Buttons found in Yungue*

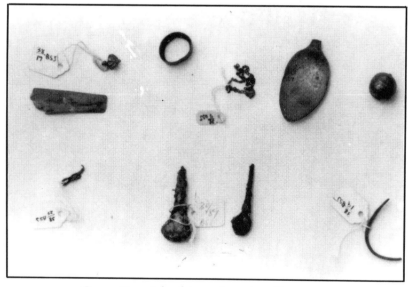

*Some Spanish objects found at Yungue*

# San Gabriel del Yungue,
# as seen by an Archaeologist

The pen may be mightier than the sword, but to judge from historic accounts dating from past centuries, important as they are to all of us, there were times when the ink ran out. Or, more likely, the penman so often was too taken up with the very real problems of daily existence in a new and difficult environment to set down all the details his or someone else's descendants - centuries later - might want to know.

About what? Well, about the precise rather than general location of where that historic settlement was established. And where and of what materials and size, and according to what floor plan the first permanent church mentioned in the record was constructed. Also, such matters as the size of those living quarters which the colonists took over from resident Indians but complained were cold, smokey, and bug-ridden. And if and how those quarters were furnished. What kinds of vessels were used for cooking and for serving meals? In general, how those first colonists and missionaries to actually settle north of today's United States-Mexico border were celebrating their new home 33 years after other Spaniards had settled in San Augustine, Florida, but 22 years *before* English settlers established themselves at Plymouth Rock.

And, as part of the close association in late sixteenth and seventeenth century New Mexico, what lasting influence did those two groups of human beings, Spaniards and Pueblo Indians, each with its own historically successful pattern of living (anthropologically their "culture") bring to bear upon the other?

## The Background

We know from the records that missionization was a primary point with the Crown and with the 10 friars (8 priests and 2 assistants) who accompanied Oñate's colonists in making that first permanent settlement in our Southwest. There also was the desire for territorial expansion and always the hope for discovery of some source of wealth, even though their earlier explorers actually had brought nothing more convincing than tall tales when they returned from the borderlands. The Crown, however, made but very little contribution of funds or equipment to the project. To the uninitiated it comes as something of a surprise to learn that it was Oñate himself, plus two opulent family members in Mexico, who were footing the bills and who in the long run would lose a fortune in the hope of finding one.

9

Oñate and his captains, on horseback, reached San Juan Pueblo on July 11, 1598, and were invited to make themselves at home. The remainder of his colonists were slowly struggling northward with 83 unwieldy oxcarts and wagons of household goods, foods, and a multitude of listed equipment, as well as over 7,000 head of horses, cattle, sheep, and goats. The five weeks and two days Oñate and his companions were to wait before the main party should appear would be devoted to visiting the various Pueblos on the Rio Grande and its tributaries, recording the Indians' oaths of allegiance to the Spanish King, and making plans for the distribution of missionaries. Necessary duties, in terms of that period in history, in spite of the fact that we can be sure (and as was later demonstrated) the Indians, as unused to the concepts of kings and kingdoms as to the Spanish language, could have had little idea of just what was going on.

On August 11th, in their last free week, Oñate's captains "began construction" (probably actually the "direction of construction") of an irrigation ditch for the "City of our Father, Saint Francis" (Hammond and Rey 1953:322). We see a reflection of Pueblo good will and at the same time an indication of the size of San Juan Pueblo in the statement that about 1500 Indians (presumably all men, for this was not a job at which Pueblo women labored) were helping the Spaniards with this ditch. As Pueblo ancestors had constructed and used irrigation ditches in the Chama Valley and on other side streams of the Rio Grande at least since A.D. 1300 and perhaps earlier (Ellis 1970, 1988), the Indians probably would have handled the project better than the Spanish officers, especially with the only implements available until the colonists' carts arrived being native-made digging sticks and perhaps stone axes for excavation and baskets or blankets for moving the soil. According to San Juan tradition, all the Spanish ditches were west of the river.

It hardly requires reading between the lines to realize that Oñate, from the beginning, had intended to establish something of an urban center, named for St. Francis, patron of the friars accompanying his party. But the only community building put up during that year, as far as we presently know, was a church. The structure, we read, was begun on Aug. 23, only 5 days after the main party of colonists reached San Juan Pueblo. Within 15 days the project was so far advanced that its dedication to St. John the Baptist was celebrated, though a few more weeks were to pass before final completion. After the ceremony, the religious play of Los Moros y los Cristianos was put on, presumably for the benefit of the Indians. Comprehension of this religious drama (still given by many communities in Spain and a few in northern New Mexico) which concentrates on the final expulsion of the Moors from Spain hardly could have been expected of the natives, but the occasion gave opportunity for display of horsemanship and of assorted weapons, presumably to the delight of both peoples.

No one today has any idea where this first church was erected or of what materials; there is neither Pueblo tradition (as far as we could learn) nor documentary record. Even the frame of a religious structure intended to accommodate the 400 male colonists, plus wives and children brought along by 130 of those men, plus an unstated number of servants (Bolton 1930:202) and, one would surmise, some Pueblo Indian guests, could not have been erected in two weeks time if stone, wood, or adobes had been used. One might guess that it would have been a temporary jacal structure of upright posts set into a trench and heavily plastered with adobe mud inside and out. Wherever the site, it probably has been many times built over in the expansion resulting from natural increase in native population and the fact that the general pattern of Pueblo layout since the 1500s has changed from one of several storied house blocks tightly enclosing a plaza to a minimally outlined plaza supplemented by widespread one story modernized homes.

It seems that history is not even clear as to whether the colonists first settled and built that initial church in San Juan Pueblo on the east side of the Rio Grande or elsewhere. Hammond and Rey (1953:17) state openly that the Spaniards' "first headquarters or capital" was founded "on the east bank of the Rio Grande and named San Juan de los Caballeros," though known to the natives then and now as Okeh (Okí). Dedication of that church to San Juan as patron certainly suggests that it should have been there. But then we read that after a few months

> ... they [the Spaniards] moved their camp to the pueblo of Yunque or Yugewinge [elsewhere spelled by the Spaniards as Yuque Yunque and Yunque Yunque and with other variations, all approximations of the actual native name of Yúnge Ouínge] which they called San Gabriel, on the left bank of the Chama where it flowed into the Rio Grande. This was a town of approximately four hundred houses and was more adequate for the needs of the Spanish forces. It remained the capital of New Mexico until Governor Don Pedro de Peralta, Oñate's successor, founded Santa Fe in 1610.                    (Hammond and Rey 1953:17).

The deduction of these two historians, that the Spaniards made their first headquarters in San Juan but moved to Yungue in the winter of 1600-1601 (France Scholes, personal communication, 1954) was based on the fact that, of the four letters sent out from the Oñate camp between 1598 and the end of 1600, one was datelined as written "at the Pueblo of San Juan" on the last day of February, 1599, one of the same year but without month mentions the writer's group being in the province of the Teguas (Tewas) but gives no dateline, and two, both similarly marked 1599, are datelined simply as "New Mexico" (Hammond and Rey 1953:427, 481, 490, 493). In contrast, we have all five letters written between March 22 nd October 2, 1601, datelined "San Gabriel" or "At the pueblo of San Gabriel" (Op. cit.:608, 672, 690, 700, 701).

However, when Don Luis de Velasco wrote that long letter covering innumerable complaints against Oñate, the camp, and the countryside, datelining it as "From the pueblo of San Gabriel, March 22, 1601," he included a puzzling statement:

> In this manner we came to a pueblo where the governor [Oñate] ordered a halt. It is the one from which I am writing to your lordship. We have been here three years, hoping to discover something of value and importance, which has not been found up to the present.    (Hammond and Rey 1953:609)

Just where had the Spaniards been quartered those three years? In San Gabriel? Hammond and Rey (1953:609, fn. 3) footnote Velasco's statement with a reiteration but no explanation:

> The expedition first settled at San Juan de los Caballeros but after a short time had moved to San Gabriel.

How can we be certain? Hopefully, we reach for *History of New Mexico*, an epic poem by Villagrá, one of Oñate's captains, published in 1610. Villagrá's eye witness accounts of much that occurred leaves us in his debt, but his only pertinent note on this question is that when they reached "a splendid pueblo" which they named San Juan, the natives came out and "shared their homes" with the newcomers (Villagrá 1933:147).

Our suggestion is that the problem is more apparent than real, though puzzling enough to warrant some lines of ethnographic clarification.

Velasco well may have been - accurately - thinking of San Juan and Yunque as two parts of a single pueblo. This certainly is done today by those "San Juan" families which live in the San Gabriel del Yunque area (some even on top of the old site). According to tradition, Yunque as a Pueblo was somewhat older than Okeh, the people of the latter earlier having lived a few miles farther up the Rio Grande but moving successively closer to and finally onto the site of Okeh as their previously occupied locations were washed out. The San Juan tribesmen today explain that the two physical entities, Yungue on the west side of the Rio Grande and Okeh on the east side of the same river, originally were, respectively, the homes of their Summer people and that of the Winter people. The two moieties today comprise the single tribe which we outsiders refer to as "San Juan." Today's natives speak of their tribe and overall site as that of "San Juan Pueblo," but they list its components as Okeh, Yungue, Pueblito (that little farm village a short distance up the Rio Grande on the west side of the river), and El Llano, the flat area of houses and small farms south of Okeh to the east of the river.

In other words, there may be several geographic divisions within a "Pueblo," just as there are numerous subdivisions or other named sections within one of our organized Anglo communities, whether the huge City of Los Angeles or the moderate sized cities of Albuquerque and Santa Fe. Simple enough, but a problem which long has confused non-Indians in relation to Pueblos including San Juan.

Early Spaniards exploring the Southwest reported clusters of sites which spoke a single language and looked to a single pueblo as the ceremonial and political center of that cluster. To those Spaniards, the cluster and associated lands became a "province." On August 3, 1598, for example, Oñate and his men had gone

> ... to the great pueblo of the Emes [Jemez]. On the 4th we went down to the other Emes pueblos. They say there are eleven altogether; we saw eight. ... On the 5th we went down one league to the last pueblo of this province.
> (Hammond and Rey 1953:322)

Very few historic Pueblos[*] have consisted of people living in but a single local habitation unit. Our best modern example is Laguna Pueblo, a tribe as such but made up of at least nine local habitation groups at some distance from each other and each with its own name: Old Laguna, New Laguna, Paguate, Paraje, Mesita, Encinal, Seama, and three post World War II additions with the tongue-in-cheek designations of New York, Philadelphia, and Chinatown. The tribal center of religion and government always has been Old Laguna. Similarly, though on a smaller scale, Acoma

---

[*]    We use the capitaled "Pueblo" to designate a people, tribe, or person of Pueblo type culture, but also use it as part of a village name: San Juan Pueblo. The non-capitalized "pueblo" should refer only to the architectural entity, but we admit that all writers are not consistent on these points.

Pueblo recognizes as its three components the villages of Acoma (on the Mesa), Acomita, and McCartys. The old site on the mesa long was the political as well as religious center, but today we casually speak of "going out to Acoma," when our destination in reality is Acomita where matters of government presently are handled in a new community center and council hall. Zuni, Isleta, Jemez, Zia, Cochiti, Tesuque, Nambí, Pojoaque, San Ildefonso, Santa Clara, and Taos all are known to have been comprised of more than one settlement or "great house" in the historic period.

One's tribe and home thus might be given as Acoma, Laguna, or San Juan, though his actual residence was in McCartys, Paguate, or Yungue (San Gabriel). Our suggestion is that Don Luis de Velasco and his companions were living at San Gabriel and recognized it as a suburb of San Juan, the center, even today, which gives its name to the entire tribe.

San Gabriel del Yungue apparently was as close a substitute as could be had for Oñate's dream of the "City of our Father, San Francisco."

A revealing comment is that of Gines de Hererra Horta who had been sent to New Mexico as "chief auditor and legal assessor to Don Juan de Oñate, governor ..." with the auxiliary group which reached San Gabriel at the end of December, 1600, when after a few uncomfortable months this official intruder, resented by Oñate, was quickly granted his request to return to Mexico. His 1601 report to the authorities, included some expectable uncomplimentary commentaries, but there was one paragraph which clearly reflects the deep disappointments against which Oñate was struggling:

> ... the governor [Oñate] wanted a town established, an alcalde named and houses built, but that the Spaniards [colonists] refused. This witness thought that the reason for this was their dissatisfaction at remaining and their desire to abandon the land because of the great deprivations they were suffering.　　　　(Hammond and Rey 1953:652)

There was little he could do about the drought which struck in the years 1600 and 1601,[*] leaving everyone hungry and some of the Indians near starvation. The small native stores of corn and a few other foods, customarily set aside by each family to hold it over some two years of dearth in crops, had been consumed when the Spaniards forced their demands for food.

---

[*]　These drought years are clearly shown in tree-ring records for the northern Rio Grande drainage. (Smiley, Stubbs, and Bannister 1953).

Some of the colonists had suggested that Oñate should have ordered a communal field planted, but apparently he did not. Was his reason the difficulties with the unruly young men who resented the absence of plentiful Spanish females, the lack of silver bars "lying on the ground," Oñate's rules against despoiling the Indians of blankets and other possessions, - and who frequently went their own way in spite of rules and punishments?

The one solution Oñate could see to the problem of the Spanish city which was not to be built was requesting the Indians who had been living in the partly ruined pueblo of Yungue to vacate that 400 room native condominium ar ' turn it over to the Spaniards as their own habitation and center. That the Indian officials agreed may reflect something of the difficulties they had been experiencing with Spaniards quartered so close within the native domain. Our uncovering of what appeared to have been an old Pueblo shrine in one room points to a few natives having remained in Yungue to work for the Spaniards in some remodeling of the original structures and possibly, at a guess, in some farm and other labors, but they could easily have lived in Okeh and walked a quarter mile to work at Yungue. Other Yungue citizens, as we think likely because of occupation date suggested by sherd types, may have left Yungue to move up the Rio Grande 4 miles to establish the farm hamlet still known as Pueblito.

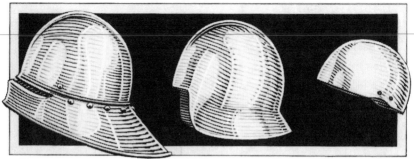

*These artist's renditions illustrate some of the possible ways the archer's helmet may have looked. Illustrations by Glen Strock.*

*Spanish military helmet found at Yungue;*
*Top: Side View, Bottom: Back View;*
*Courtesy of Museum of NM, Neg. Nos. 46664 & 46665*

# AN ARCHAEOLOGICAL SUMMARY Of SAN GABRIEL del YUNGUE (to date)

## Early Work: Important Bits and Pieces

It was in 1944 that Dr. Edgar Lee Hewett, Director of the Museum of New Mexico and of the School of American Research, called in Marjorie Tichy (now Lambert), his curator of archaeology, and asked her to go out for a little personal investigation at the possible site of San Gabriel del Yungue. Hewett long had been an admirer of Adolph Bandelier, the late 19th century archaeologist-ethnologist who believed in considering, where possible, regional archival background (often from his own translations) in the light of evaluating native oral history, architecture, and artifacts. Piecing together the notes of early Spaniards from the Coronado expedition as recorded by Castañeda in 1541, Villagrá's epic poem of 1610 covering Oñate's colony, and what official records of Oñate's difficult venture then were available, Bandelier stated simply that:

> When Oñate came in 1598, he moved directly to San Juan, established his camp there, and proceeded to found San Gabriel, on the opposite bank of the Rio Grande. (Bandelier 1890:124, fn. 1. Also see data under Yungue, Yungue-Yungue, Yuge-uin-ge, and San Gabriel, Bandelier 1890:311; 1892:31, 36 fn. 1, 58, 59, 123, 330 fn. 1).

By 1944 Bandelier's suggested location of San Gabriel across the Rio Grande from San Juan was marked by a very few Indian dwellings on the western and southwestern peripheries. The main ruin, according to Tichy, had

> ... been reduced, through cultivation, to an irregular quadrangle with breaks or openings, on the southeast and northwest. A cienega or pond, is said by the Indians to have once been a part of the depression that forms the center. In recent years it was drained to bring the area under cultivation. Remnants of a rather large adobe and rubble building and a well that appears to be recent, occupy the top center of

the east mound. San Juan Indians say that this structure was occupied by Spanish-Americans until about 1916, when the inhabitants were evicted from Indian land.

Indian informants maintain that San Gabriel Mission occupied the southwest point of the site where an Indian dwelling now stands. The family living here did not permit any digging. (Tichy 1944:222)

Because of war time conditions, only one San Juan man and at times his wife could be procured to aid in the brief sampling excavations. A stratigraphic test on the northeast side and a second test on the southwest side of the same mound produced little except evidence that a large portion of the original prominence had been destroyed by farming and "rather large scale adobe making projects on the part of nearby residents."

A test trench northeast into the main mound uncovered sherds, bones, some stone artifacts, and also room walls badly damaged by adobe making operations. The remaining wall of the first room stood only 1 foot above the floor, but a foundation of large undressed stones beneath the wall could be seen. Walls of the adjoining room stood 4 feet above the old floor, some discolored plaster still remained on one wall, and wood, which appeared to have been a post or fragments of roofing, remained and was saved but turned out to be undatable. Two other rooms also were uncovered each measuring approximately 12 X 7 feet. In the fill near the floor were local Tewa sherds of Biscuit and Sankawi Black-on-white and some contemporary Glaze-decorated sherds characteristic of pueblos farther south in the Rio Grande drainage between A.D. 1350 and 1700. The latter presumably were from trade vessels.

Although no article of Spanish origin had come to light during this work, Tichy's deduction from the single week of excavation was that this site did, indeed, give the impression that it could have been that of San Gabriel. Her final point was

> ... the absolute necessity of marking and preventing any more destruction to the site, which may sometime settle the important historical and archaeological question of the site of the first capital of New Mexico. (Tichy 1944:224)

In 1942 or '43 Stephen Trujillo, a member of San Juan Pueblo, had accidentally kicked up a fragment from a bronze object with a raised decoration on one side as he crossed a field near where Tichy's small excavations later would be made. Three years later, he gave the metal fragment to Dr. C.S. Diefendorf of Santa Fe, who long had admired it. Dr. Diefendorf, believing this to be of importance in establishing the site as that of Yungue, handed it on to Marjorie Tichy, who arranged for metallographic examination of it by specialists C.G. Fink and P. Polushkin. They identified it as probably having been a fragment of the bell which might have hung in San Gabriel Mission (Tichy 1946; Fink and Polushkin 1946). A second opinion prevalent in the 1950s was that the fragment had come from a bronze object too small to have been a mission bell but could have been from a mortar such as used for grinding medicinal materials or spices. Such a bronze mortar was included in the inventory of items Oñate brought north from Mexico. (Hammond and Rey 1953:253).

Later learning that the entire site was in danger of total destruction through extensive adobe-making operations, Tichy and another Museum employee went out to see how bad the damage might be at "what is believed to be the first capital of New Mexico."

> Unfortunately, we found the destruction only too real. A bulldozer had been used, and the great sweep made by it leaves somewhat less than half of the only remaining mound of any size. A considerable number of rooms were destroyed, including all of those excavated in 1944 by the Museum of New Mexico. Indeed, since this mound consisted of old adobe dwellings, the very walls have been remade into adobes which are now going into new buildings elsewhere.
> Large quantities of pottery and other cultural items, and human skeletal remains, now crushed and destroyed, could be seen. Mrs. Virginia Jennings and the writer made a collection of this broken material. The most important find was a badly corroded mass of metal which appears to be chain mail.     (Tichy 1946:324)

In response to a letter concerning "this archaeological and historical disaster" mailed to the United Pueblos Agency in Albuquerque, a representative sent to investigate the report met with the Governor of San Juan Pueblo. The Governor chanced to own the land on which the ruins lay, and his explanation was that the Indians had not understood that any harm was being done and in the future would "get in touch with the Museum before heavy digging or cultivation is begun in the vicinity of the ruin." Unfortunately, this did not mark the end of cultivation, adobe making, and even construction on the site of Yungue, but it did minimize it.

In 1951, José Abeyta, the Summer cacique of San Juan Pueblo, while making adobe bricks on his own land,[*] came across the crown of what originally had been an iron helmet. He already had torn down an Indian dwelling of several rooms[**] on top of the west mound of old Yungue, planning to replace it with a house for his daughter.

The construction material was to be his adobes, formed of earth dug close to the north edge of the razed structure and definitely into the old west mound.

At the bottom of his adobe pit (ca. 3 x 4 feet across and 4 feet deep) he accidentally struck and broke one of the stone griddles long used by Pueblo women when making paper bread *(guayaves)*. Beneath the griddle he found a large culinary jar (Sapawe Micaceous ribbed in type), also broken by his blow. Inside the jar, which probably had been left setting on a Spanish period floor with the griddle as a lid, was what he referred to as "the old hat." Nested within the "hat" was "a small cup," apparently (by description, as one of the local children had admired and appropriated it) of Glaze VI Red decorated with black glaze paint. This type dates at approximately A.D. 1550-1700.

Thinking the strange "hat" might have some importance, Abeyta took it to Henry Kramer, who for many years had run the local general store. Kramer "paid Abeyta something for it" and then at once brought it to Santa Fe to present to the Museum of New Mexico. With Hewett's authorization, Tichy sent the piece to Harold L. Peterson, Chief of Historical Investigations, National Park Service, in Washington D.C. Peterson identified it as having been a crested but fairly flat archer's type of head covering known as a *salade*. It was reported to have probably dated a hundred years before Oñate founded his capital, presumably having been among some of the

---

[*]  In the old Pueblo concept, land was parceled out by a leader as required for use of an individual in providing for his family, but should that use cease, the land went back to the Pueblo for redistribution. Through acculturation, the Pueblo people have come to think of private land ownership more in Spanish American and Anglo terms, but it still is rather a "use permission" in that reservation and grant lands actually are held in trust by the United States government for usage by tribal members. They can not be sold to outsiders, though today those lands, in use or not, commonly are handed down within a family and can be bought and sold within the tribe.

[**]  This well may have been the large adobe and rubble structure photographed by Forrest and incorrectly identified in his history (Forrest 1929:42) as the first Spanish church. As far as we have evidence, no church ever occupied that position. As the remains of that building were on the surface of the mound and the jar containing the helmet was 4 feet beneath the surface, the adobe and rubble structure quite certainly dated after Spanish abandonment of San Gabriel.

second hand equipment collected in Spain for use of the "Conquistadores" in the New World.

This identification would have depicted the head covering as originally having been equipped with neck pieces but never with a brim (Lambert 1952).

Peterson showed photographs of the helmet (Fig. 1) to two specialists in the Metropolitan Museum of New York, and both agreed with his identification. A third specialist (not associated with that museum) differed in his opinion of the specific type of helmet represented, suggesting that originally a brim had been attached to the crown. To quote from Peterson's commentary:

> The fact that the date of the manufacture of the helmet is perhaps a century earlier than the establishment of San Gabriel by Don Juan de Oñate should cause no concern. The men who led such expeditions had to supply much of the equipment themselves in order to obtain the appointment as captain-general and governor of the expedition and conquered territory. They were, therefore interested in obtaining this material as cheaply as possible and consequently much obsolete equipment was purchased. Also, since armor was relatively scarce in Mexico, pieces that dated back to the early Conquest could well be expected to have seen service until they were completely worn out. Thus, there is ample reason for a helmet of 1480-1510 to be found in the site of a settlement of 1598.        (Peterson 1952:286-287)

Peterson found no trace of iron remaining in the helmet; what was left was merely rust. Consequently, the piece is exceedingly fragile and has been given careful conservation treatment to prevent further deterioration. For a time the helmet was exhibited in the Palace of the Governors (Museum of New Mexico) in Santa Fe. In late years, however, it has been kept packed away in their vault of historic items to insure the greatest protection possible. This "oldest piece of armor" ever found in the United States (Lambert 1952:86) is too important to all Americans, Indians and non-Indians alike, for any chances to be taken with it.

We can all echo Lambert's (Tichy's) closing comment:

> It is interesting to remember at this point that the two most important discoveries at San Gabriel del Yungue [as of 1952] have not been made by trained scientists but by Indians. Highest praise should be given José Abeyta, who has shown

~~his wisdom and astuteness in public affairs for years, for his~~
awareness that something unearthed might be of profound
value.

It is regrettable that so much of this important ruin has
been damaged beyond saving. It is a historic locality which,
unfortunately, is receiving [little] attention [and] too late.

(Lambert 1952:87)

But - fortunately - there was more left of the site of San Gabriel del Yungue than anyone realized in 1952. In the spring of 1959, I was surprised to
receive from the then Governor of San Juan Pueblo a letter requesting that
I bring the University of New Mexico Archaeological Field School to excavate at San Gabriel. This was the first time any Pueblo had requested archaeological work on their premises, and I hurried to look over the site.

Villagrá's description states that the pueblo was an irregular quadrangle
with four corner entrances to the single plaza. The Spaniards built no for-
tifications but manned those entrances (Villagrá, quoted by Bandelier
1892:59; fn. 1.). The pueblo contained about "400 houses which the
Spaniards adapted for their living quarters" (Hammond and Rey 1953:639).

What I found on first inspection was a west mound, the highest local
elevation, and a much lower east mound, the two connected into a horseshoe shape enclosing the old plaza area where a big underground kiva is
said to have been located. The pond of water of which Lambert was told
would have been runoff which collected in the kiva depression. A corn field
and small apple orchard now occupy that space. The west mound, according to San Juan tradition, had been the barracks of Oñate's military contingent. On top and more or less toward its center was a neat little modern
house with hand carved posts supporting the front porch. This was the
residence of Anna Maria, daughter of José Abeyta, and her Spanish
American husband, Nicolas Salazar, a member of the House of Represen-
tatives of New Mexico in 1985. Their home was to be enlarged and at its
front, where the mound sloped downward to the north, we were told, a rose
garden or possibly a swimming pool was planned. The south end of this
west mound gently descended to disappear in farm lands belonging to the
Martinez family. Yungue's central plaza, at the eastern base of the west
mound, had been planted to corn by the Salazars.

The north end of the west mound curves around to the east and beyond,
where it had been cut through by an irrigation ditch of historic period, it
continued to the south as what we designated the east mound. That elevation sloped southward to disappear in a low area that had been leveled,
planted to corn, and irrigated for some years by Lee Montoya. East of it at

a distance of perhaps 1/4 mile ran the Rio Grande, its banks freshened with cottonwood, Russian olive, and willow but far from devoid of mosquitos. (Refer to Map. Fig. 4)

Access to the Yungue area was a rough little side road which left Highway 285 (to Ojo Caliente and on into Colorado via Antonito) immediately after crossing a narrow bridge to the west side of the Rio Grande. This road paralleled the river southward, passing the Montoya house and then the foundations which marked the location of the old railroad station that had served the once famous "Chili Line," the narrow gauge Denver and Rio Grande Railway. Here the dirt road split, the right fork turning sharply westward to pass the Martinez farm and house and then curving up the west mound to the Salazar residence.

If there ever was a southern house block to make a rectangle of the horseshoe shape, nothing of it now was visible. A low south mound, however, certainly could have been largely leveled before and/or after the Martinez house, farm buildings, and field were built.

As the west mound was the most visible and also the most threatened by current San Juan Pueblo expansion and modernization, we decided to begin our excavations there. Mr. Salazar told us that at one time he had started to level this mound for a field but gave up the operation when he realized that ruins composed a good part of its height. At another time, he had staked the north area of the mound to be used as a pasture for livestock; we found not only his old posts but those from an earlier period when someone else had tried the same plan.

So — with 40 to 60 students per season, 4 to 6 student assistants (crew chiefs) under my direction, and a varying number of San Juan men hired to help with the heavier shoveling and wheelbarrow work, we began uncovering some 100 rooms on three superimposed levels between the Salazar House and the present west mound.

## Culture Succession in Yungue's West Mound

Our excavations, inaugurated in June, 1959, ran from an arbitrary line drawn 30 feet north of the then small Salazar residence located on the highest point of this mound, to the north end of the mound as then existent.

The elevation had grown up from the original field level as the result of occupation by three distinct peoples who settled here successively, all before the "modern period." "Modern" could be defined as opening with initial construction of the Salazar house in the 1940s. Our working designations for the groups which had left the cultural remains we uncovered were (top to bottom) (1) Spanish American, most recent, (2) Oñate's Colonial Spanish following close on sixteenth century use and renovations by the Pueblo people of Yungue Ouinge, and (3) Late Prehistoric into Early

Historic Pueblo. Pueblo construction here (to judge from datable pottery types) apparently had begun in the late 1200s or early 1300s, and the mound had risen as the result of habitations falling into decay and collapsing, new structures then being built on the old remains. Reversing that trend, bulldozing efforts in modern times would have removed some of the height and width of the mound and somewhat mixed the deposits of potsherds from preceding centuries. That mixing of debris was further accentuated by excavation of pits dug in some of the old deposits to accommodate burials made by later peoples. Still more pits eventually would be required for the secondary burial of certain of those remains when encountered by later peoples during construction of their own domiciles. We came across a number of such re-interments, one carefully folded into a newspaper carrying a Dick Tracy cartoon strip. Modern - yes, but we know that the original concept of interment in ash heaps or old habitation mounds long antedates the acquired custom of laying them away in sanctified ground.

We began our work with students and Indian employees stationed at 5 foot intervals on both sides of the mound, trenching toward its center at ground (field) level to locate the stubs of the most peripheral walls of which there was still evidence. From those we could outline walls for a part or the entire distance to the top of the mound. Once at the top, we immediately located, only two inches below soft topsoil, a smooth level floor, whitened and solidified with lime or gypsum. Careful work in separating the layers showed that it had been re-plastered six times, as the surface wore through. No walls associated with this floor were standing.

Some similar floors were found toward the south of this mound (above rooms 51, 52, 53, and 56) as we cleaned the surface of weeds and low bushes. Where any remains of related walls still could be seen, they were identified as built of adobe bricks. This top layer represented the last appreciable occupancy of this mound, the families which had built their small homes here in the later nineteenth-into-twentieth century are known to have been Spanish Americans. Technically, they were trespassers, and in the 1920s they were asked by the Indians to remove themselves from the native reservation. The request became an order after trespass investigations by the Pueblo Land Board in the later years of that decade and into the early 1930s. Lack of evidence of such surface level floors in the central section of the mound is no indication that there had been no Spanish American houses there. The bulldozing operations already mentioned would have removed the evidence. Farther to the north, we encountered trash pits and/or root cellars of the same phase. These had been dug into the fill of older rooms (23, 28, 32, 39, 46) and left packed with junk of the present century such as discarded old shoes, bottles, pieces of broken household and field equipment, and newspapers.

When digging operations reached 8 or 10 inches below topsoil at the crest of the mound, we began to come across coursed adobe walls. These had belonged to renovated native-built rooms (each indicated by a number on the map) occupied by Oñate's Spanish colonists. Almost every room rested on a narrow cobblestone foundation such as used by Pueblos of the Rio Grande Valley since about A.D. 1350. The cobbles had been laid in lines of two or occasionally three stones across and only one in height, in a shallow trench or in some cases on the ground surface of that period. The stones were the base on which the well-worked adobe mud for walls would be patted into place, row after row, each row laid up by emptying successive baskets or vessels full of similar clay and soil mix onto the previous row, then leaving the layer to "set" enough to support the next row before it was added. Most of these walls, averaged 8 to 12 inches in thickness. Today they stood only 6 to 18 inches above the associated floors, the upper parts having eroded into fill or been cut off by the bulldozing.

Nor were the floors all at one level or finished in the same fashion. That of room 15, for example, only 8 inches below the present wall top, had been covered with a layer of smooth clay plaster and then toughened and blackened with animal blood, the favorite technique during the period of first construction in this houseblock, but still used into the 1930s in some pueblos. In contrast, room 17, buried under 3 feet of wind blown and packed silt when we uncovered it, showed only a partial remaining floor, well solidified but without blood coating. At the time of our work, the west wall of that room was 12 inches high and the south wall measured 11-14 inches, but only 6-8 inches above floor level remained of the north wall. In one half of room 13, the smooth adobe floor was higher than in either room 15 or 17. No definite floor could be found in a few rooms, such as 11 and 12. What once was there evidently had weathered away, perhaps when the roof decayed after abandonment. One can expect some abandoned houses in a pueblo, as in our modern towns, even while most of the rooms still are occupied and, hence, kept in repair.

The occupation level we are describing is that which the San Juan people refer to as having been taken as a "garrison" for the Spanish colonist-soldiers. Most of the west mound rooms of this phase were rectangular in shape and of approximately 6 x 8 or 7 x 10 feet, providing a floor space of some 50 to 70 square feet. The axes of a few ran east-west, but more in the area excavated measured longer north-south. An occasional room was almost square. Except at the north end, we had clear evidence of seven to eight contiguous rooms having been constructed per east-west transect. There were no entrances from the outside and very few between rooms, which means that they could have been entered only by ladders descending through a hatchway in each roof. The lack of identifiable firepits or fireboxes except in a very few of this group proves that the Spaniards were not cooking in those rooms. Lack of a firepit in a Pueblo room commonly is taken as an indication that the room was used for storage.

Ground floor storage rooms are known for various prehistoric and historic sites throughout the Pueblo area, many Hopi Indians living on their northern Arizona mesas still continue this custom. Our best late prehistory example for the northern Rio Grande is found in the very large ancestral Tewa site of Sapawe (closely related to Yungue according to Tewa tradition), 2 miles southeast of El Rito in the Chama drainage. There our own excavations (made in the years directly after those at Yungue) showed that the first story rooms of one plaza originally were provided with well constructed fireboxes sunken into the floor against the inner surface of the east outside wall. One or more ventilation holes were made in that wall to help urge the smoke upward and out the combined entrance and smoke hole in the roof. Some time later, however, those first floor Sapawe fireboxes were filled with ash and neatly covered over with floor plaster. At the same time, it seems, a second story of living, cooking, and grinding rooms was built above what were now banks of first story storage rooms.

We have no documentary statement whatsoever as to how many stories made up the pueblo of Yungue when it was taken over by the Spaniards. But the fact that some of the west mound room walls uncovered by our crew reached more than 6 feet above field (base) level and that those rooms all had been completely packed with fill which must have come from copious sources other than their own roofs strongly suggests that in the sixteenth century Yungue was at least two or three stories high. Perhaps considerably more, like the multistoried great pueblos of the Rio Grande and Pecos drainage, as seen and described by the pre-Oñate Spanish explorers. Had the surface of our west mound not been subjected to an unstated amount of bulldozing, an estimate of original Yungue height would have been much easier, though erosion over three and a half centuries still would have left uncertainties. But if the natives and later the Spaniards were not cooking and heating with firepits or fire boxes in the majority of the Yungue first story rooms they must have been living at least one story above them.

Architecturally the contiguous west mound houses that we uncovered and classified as having been occupied by Oñate's "soldier-colonists" could not be said to have differed from those occupied by Pueblo families of the Upper Rio Grande during the same time period. What indications had we, then, as archaeologists, that the San Juan tradition of these having been taken over for use as barracks by the unmarried colonists was based on fact?

The answer is simple. Artifacts.

Most of the artifact material here and elsewhere in Yungue, as shown by our work, consisted of local sherds and occasional stone implements, whole or broken. Most of those implements were metates, manos, and stone axes, none very diagnostic as to period. The sherds, as usual, told us much more. From the surface to the floors of these "upper" houses we were excavating, the greatest percentages of decorated sherds were of Biscuit A and Biscuit B, known to more or less overlap in time through a span from A.D. 1375 to 1550. Fair numbers of the two late Rio Grande glaze-decorated pottery types, 5 or E, and 6 or F, also appeared. These were produced primarily in the Galisteo Basin south of Santa Fe, in the Pecos area, or in the Middle Rio Grande drainage between Albuquerque and La Bajada Hill. They were widely traded. The two types overlapped in time and in some cases one or the other but not both are thought to have been made within certain restricted areas. Their combined dates run from A.D. 1475 to 1700 when glaze decoration was dropped in favor of matte paint ware.

Our time span for major use of the west mound, then, by natives or outsiders, could be said to run from about A.D. 1400 at least into the 1600s. But we must go farther. Three pieces of Majolica[*] ware were found in the fill of west mound rooms, between the surface and the floors which mark the bottom of the occupation level we are discussing. During early trenching in the approximate area where room 4 later would be outlined, one sherd of Majolica was found 2 feet below the contemporary (1959) surface. Another was found in the fill of room Y,[**] 2 feet below the surface level. The third lay in a level of fill at 12 to 20 inches below the top of the east wall of room 12. The Majolica brought by colonists into the Southwest was glazed all over with a tin glaze and hence contrasts with Southwestern late prehistoric "glaze-decorated wares" on which the glaze paint, consisting principally of lead, often a little copper, plus flux and coloring matter (Hawley 1931; Hawley and Hawley 1938) was used only for a part of the design work. Some of the colorful Majolica sherds found in Yungue were of Spanish and some of early historic Mexican manufacture; they are dateable and, as we might expect, those from San Gabriel were found to have been made in the sixteenth century. They would have been primarily from vessels in the household equipment of both the secular and the religious

---

[*]    Pronounced My-ól-ica.

[**]   Indian rooms or parts of rooms in the west mound were designated by numbers, and those of the next floor above (Spanish use level) by letters of the alphabet. In some cases, designations were combined or parts of a single room received separate designations until the relationship of areas should become clear. Following our discussion of the history of rooms and occupations by the three cultural groups involved does require reference to our maps.

leaders in Oñate's entourage. Contemporary local pottery vessels would have been used by the less opulent members of his party and also by servants brought or locally hired for kitchen work or other labor.

A number of metal fragments from worn-out vessels and implements also appeared in the fill of these Spanish phase rooms, between the floor and the 1959 surface. When such finds, including the Majolica sherds, are found in room fill rather than on the floor, one must assume that they fell with the eroding and decaying remains of second or possibly even third story rooms, the wall and roof material of which, over the years, would collapse into the lower floor rooms beneath them.

In contrast, no Majolica sherds and very few bits of Spanish metal were found in work on the lowest or bottom floor occupation level.

We do not claim that the west mound structures taken for occupation by Oñate's men were constructed by the Spaniards. To judge from what is said in the Oñate papers, the Spaniards simply moved into the rooms when the native Indians moved out of them. There is, however, appreciable material evidence that the upper parts of the walls of some of the west mound rooms first occupied by the Indians were cut off and the debris pushed into the hollow of the room to provide a base on which to build up a new floor and walls for rooms to be used by the Spaniards. Some of this could have happened when the Indians did a stint of reconstruction of their old site in pre-Spanish times but our impression is that more was done in renovation for Spanish use. Certainly when one discovers a number of walls more or less evenly cut across at a certain general level and some difference in color of clay from which the walls were built *above* that level, he is inclined to surmise that reconstruction was carried on. Our opinion when we had completed what we could of excavations in this mound was that this work had been done after the Spaniards had taken over the pueblo of Yungue, probably as a result of their complaint that the old Pueblo rooms were smokey and contaminated with bedbugs (Hammond and Rey 1953:656, 669). In a very few cases some of this work may have been done by the Spaniards, themselves, for we have some evidence that a few adobe bricks were used, as they were in sixteenth century Spain and north Africa. The great preponderance of the construction work, however, was of coursed adobe with which this group of Pueblo people long had been acquainted. We read that:

> As for personal service, when they need to repair any
> houses or walls, they send for Indian women to do the work,
> as they are the plasterers and builders.
>
> (Hammond and Rey 1953:656)

The first story and first built structures, those representing the original construction of late Pueblo III into Pueblo IV (A.D.1250-1550) at the bottom of the west mound, were quite easy to recognize, once we had uncovered a few. They were of coursed adobe, as might be expected, but they usually *did not have* foundations of cobbles or of other stones, as was characteristic for walls of the later built rooms above. The interior wall surface in Level III usually was plastered and often finished with a white surface of clay or gypsum, favored throughout the Pueblo country and practical from the standpoint of making the usually rather dark interior of a room, without light and ventilated only by a small wall opening and the ceiling hatchway, appreciably brighter. This was not a matter of cheer but of being able to see one's work. Some of the northern rooms of that earlier period had north-south walls that certainly did not meet their supposedly east-west walls at a 90 degree angle. This was growth by accretion rather than planning. But most rooms were rectangular with approximately 80 square feet of floor space.

The long walls of the rooms built above that bottom story and occupied first by the Indians but later taken for Spanish use, ran quite directly north and south. Of the comparable walls represented by those cut down and rebuilt for Spanish occupation, the more northern were set at an angle about 30 degrees off from those below.

Many of the floors of this earliest construction were black, probably from a surfacing of animal blood. In room C a sunken firebox had been constructed at the center of its northern wall; later it came to be partially covered by a second level wall, part of the rebuilding project.

Sherds were much fewer beneath floors of the middle occupation stage (Pueblo followed by Oñate's colonists) than above them. The highest pottery percentage for the earliest (bottom) rooms was of culinary ware, mostly in the popular category of Pueblo IV Sapawe Micaceous Washboard. Second came Biscuit A and third Biscuit B, which would lead us to think of a time level of about A.D. 1425 were it not for the occasional presence of Sankawi Black-on-cream and Potsuwi'i[*] Incised. Those carry us to A.D. 1500 if we think in terms of even a scanty overlap. No Majolica sherds were found and almost no metal fragments. Little pertaining to metates was seen below middle occupation period floors, which fits with the concept that the house owners had not moved to any great distance but merely to a new, slightly higher, and undoubtedly fresher floor level. The number of broken manos left behind in the debris was not far different from the count of those

---

[*]   Pronounced Pot-sue-wé-e.

left in the debris from the Pueblo-into-Spanish period occupation. Metates, heavy and slow to make, and lasting much longer than manos, are one thing; manos, which require but a fraction of the work before they actually can be used in corn grinding, and have little more use than any unworked stone after being broken, are another.

Bone as well as stone implements were in considerably greater abundance in the debris of lowest (oldest) rooms than above, which again reinforces the supposition that the natives who had constructed the bottom story houses had picked up their household goods and transported all of it that still seemed usable to their new homes in Okeh, San Juan itself, or perhaps to Pueblito, when the Spaniards took over. Test pits below the floors of these bottom rooms indicate there had been no earlier structures here.

To briefly summarize the west mound sequence, we can say that the bottom level represents pure Pueblo Culture, dating between A.D. 1300 or 1350 and 1500. The second level of occupation began with reconstruction of the west mound houses about 1500 and closed with the Spaniards taking over those structures for their own use probably in 1600-1601. A few of the old bottom level structures may also, with a little rebuilding, have been used by the Spaniards. The uppermost level of occupation, at the top surface of the mound, represents Spanish American squatters of late nineteenth - early twentieth century.

*Three whole Indian vessels dug up at Yungue*

*Aerial view of entire Yungue site*

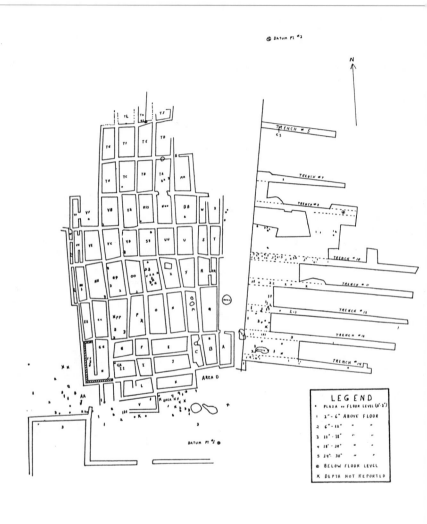

*Distribution of Metal at Yungue — Summer, 1962*

*Medal, front view*
*7/8 inch length, 5/8 inch width*

*Medal, back view*

# The East Mound, Then and Since

In 1959 we set some of the students to start excavation at the upper (north) end of the East Mound. We continued there in 1960. Skipping the north mound was intentional because it had been so bulldozed that one could not definitely locate it from the present surface, though it is quite possible that bottom floors outlined by wall stubs still may be present at a depth. On its southern edge, wherever that was, it now melded into the cultivated corn field which, with a small apple orchard, occupied what originally had been the Yungue plaza. The stub walls of the north house block might be traceable if one went below plough line, but such work would have temporarily ruined that portion of the planted field, and we had no permission to work in that location.

Initially, it was impossible to know the limits of the East Mound, though it was easily apparent that it sloped gently from north to south but evened off at field and plaza level some distance before reaching the little access road which led past the Montoya and Martinez places to the Salazar house topping the West Mound. The crest of the ridge lay just west of the badly eroded remains of a twentieth century irrigation ditch on the east side of which the terrain gently sloped into the uncultivated field. We roughly divided the northern end of all this into "sections," assigned students to those partitions, and started them digging test pits down to sterile soil. What we needed was some inkling of how the house block lay.

Our first few shovelsful of earth verified Mr. Montoya's admission that he had used the upper portion of the ridge for his adobe pit, the washed-down old walls in that area providing excellent clayey soil which, with water, would make the desired mix for filling a wooden adobe-mold many a hundred times. Sun-drying such "bricks" was all that was needed to ready them for being laid, with mud mortar, into walls in the technique introduced into New Mexico by seventeenth century Spaniards.

We have mentioned the most common prehistoric-into-historic Rio Grande construction technique, coursed adobe patted into place. A second old Pueblo construction technique used in this region and in some others, was roughly hand-shaping masses of a stiff clay mix shaped into "turtlebacks" some 12-13 inches long, 7 inches wide, and 4 inches thick. These could be laid, like bricks, across a wall or its foundation in adobe-mud mortar. The old native houses of Yungue illustrate use of both these pre-Columbian techniques.

The light brown sterile soil (containing no cultural remains) of the valley floor was found to be no more than 2 feet below the rough bottom of the washed out old irrigation ditch, which apparently had been run through a low pre-Spanish mound of discarded household debris.[*] As house walls came to light in some of our test pits and trenches, we abandoned the exploratory "areas" and concentrated on outlining and excavating a long grid of rooms running in a double and sometimes triple line down the ridge (see photo map Fig. 3).

But our elation had to be tempered. Before we could devote our major attention to the architecture and artifacts primary to our stated program of investigation, we had to struggle with the problem of intrusive burials which had been inserted into the debris deposit and, as we were to learn, similarly into the fill of some of the abandoned house block rooms.

All we knew of the dating of those interments was that they must have been made after the opening date for Sankawi Black-on-cream pottery (ca. A.D. 1525-1600) and also quite certainly after the Spaniards had given up occupation of San Gabriel del Yungue as the result of Peralta being sent up from Mexico to take over Oñate's position and move the remaining colonists to a new location. That takes us to the founding of Santa Fe in 1610.

Ages of the individuals buried here ranged from infancy to adulthood, the majority having been children or youths. This is not surprising when we recall that even into this century infant and child mortality has run high for Pueblo groups. The bodies of some and probably all of the corpses had been placed in the flexed position so long favored by the Anasazi for interments, but in most cases the remains we encountered were incomplete, an arm, leg, hands or feet, numbers of ribs, and even portions of the skulls being missing. The reason was not difficult to fathom: the weight of a moving bulldozer, of which the tracks were quite visible approximately 12 inches below the present surface but only a few inches above most of the burials, had broken, disturbed, and thereby lost many bones. We could not be certain whether placing grave goods with the body had been customary in that period or not because though we found no artifacts with most of the burials, a Sankawi Black-on-cream bowl had been placed over the head of a child as if for protection, and a Biscuit-Sankawi whole bowl was found

---

[*]     Such deposits are referred to by archaeologists as dumps or "middens," but are respectfully spoken of as "ash piles" and held to be semi-sacred areas by Pueblo people because they are composed of the remains of household fires, sherds from broken house wares, broken stone and bone artifacts, moldering baskets, and other perishable articles closely associated with the ancestors. In the prehistoric Southwest human remains also sometimes came to rest in the "ash piles." The more conservative Pueblos place prayer offerings on their ash piles for appropriate occasions, and outsiders are not permitted to set foot on their surfaces.

with another interment. We never were certain whether the partial vessels or large sherds found in some graves had been intentionally placed in position or merely had been present in the debris-fill into which the grave pit was dug. Most of the remains apparently were without grave goods except for some remnants of matting in which the body had been laid away.

We were not happy in discovering that the East Mound, like the west, had become a burial ground after the houses were abandoned, for we knew that the northern Tewa are but little less distressed than the Navajo in disturbance of their dead. Moreover, removing the bones (later to be returned to the Pueblo for interment elsewhere) with due care delayed progress in our stated concentration on architecture and artifacts representing the period of Spanish use and occupation of this site. Where had the Spanish officer-leaders lived? Where was their permanent church? Where would one find the bones of the cattle, sheep, and horses brought up from Mexico, and where were the considerable remains of Spanish-made crockery, glass, and the widely assorted metal objects listed in the inventories of what Oñate's group brought into New Mexico?

We actually were closer to those finds than we thought, but first we must make our careful way through uncovering the 30 East Mound ground floor rooms we had outlined. Their line, two to three rooms wide (east walls sometimes missing) had run down the western side of the low ridge. Walls were 9 to 10 inches thick; present height of the walls varied from 2 or 3 feet to over 5 feet. All these rooms were packed to the brim with "fill" containing plentiful sherds, charcoal, ash, soil, some stone, a few turtlebacks, a few animal bones, and a scattering of broken stone and bone implements. Alignment (see photograph map) strongly suggested that all had not been constructed at the same time but in at least two spurts of building. The size of each room was much as in the West Mound, but here opposing walls commonly were several inches from being the same length. That the structure had been more than one story in height, with living quarters on the second floor, was surmised when the floors were cleared and very few firepits could be identified. One firebox 19 inches wide and 21 inches long was uncovered close against the inside of the north wall of room 20.

The earliest sherds in the East Mound debris, as in that of the West Mound, were Santa Fe and Wiyo Black-on-whites, never numerous but definitely indicating that occupation of this site as a whole went back to some time between A.D. 1200 and 1350. The great preponderance of sherds were of Biscuit A and Biscuit B (Abiquiu and Bandelier Black-on-white: A.D. 1350 or 1375 to 1500 or 1550, as usually dated). There also was a little Potsuwi'i Incised (1425-1525 or later) and its usual companion, Sankawi Black-on-cream (1500-1600+). The two early decorated types would have preceded Spanish occupation; the two later types came into vogue shortly before and during the Spanish period.

The associated native cooking ware was Micaceous culinary, some finished with a ribbed exterior but more classified by the descriptive term "smeared-washboard-indented" style. Its most common variant showed the pinched indentations produced in construction but then largely obliterated into a somewhat rough and lightly granular surface (A.D. 1250 - post 1700) (Mera 1935; Stubbs and Stallings 1953; Ellis 1964; Breternitz 1966). There also was a constant small percentage of Glaze-decorated ware which had been produced between A.D. 1350 and 1700 and in the main received through trade with clusters of outside Pueblos, though we had some evidence (Johnson 1961) that one variant could have been made in San Juan Pueblo itself. The Glaze V and VI (E and F: 1600-1700) sherds from these rooms would have been contemporaneous with the latest use of this house block, as also could be said for the Kapo Black and San Juan Red, which first appeared about 1515-1600. Our excavations had proceeded intentionally in 6 inch levels, with rare exceptions, because with the apparent late utilization of this area for deposition of debris and burials in the room fill and in the ash mound immediately to the east, the mixed association of key pottery types representing different periods could only be expected. The bulldozing and ditch digging of modern times compounded that confusion.

The artifacts we found, an occasional mano (handstone for grinding) or mano fragment, a broken metate (milling stone) of vesicular basalt, an arrow point or a drill fashioned from chert or other relatively local mineral, lithics (flakes of stone which could be used for scraping or cutting but had not been intentionally shaped), a bone bead or two, a hollow and perforated bone "turkey call" used by hunters, and a number of whole and broken bone awls, probably used in making coiled baskets, provided a little insight into the daily lives of the Indians who had lived on the East Mound before the Spaniards took over Yungue. We also were finding a moderate number of badly oxidized metal fragments among the sherds. Unfortunately, such fragments rarely could be identified as to the artifacts of which they once had been a part; the majority were too small or too corroded, even for recognition by the specialist, Art Woodward, to whom they were submitted.

Those metal fragments still were clear evidence of Spanish contact. Another significant find was the one leg broken from a typical three-legged Mexican-style metate. The grinding stones of our native Southwestern peoples all were designed without legs, but those brought up from Mexico by the Indian servants who accompanied many of the settlers would have been very similar in shape to those still used in villages south of our border today.

Yes, the houses we had been excavating on the upper East Mound certainly had been occupied during the Spanish period - but by whom?

Possibly in small part by those local San Juan Indians retained by the Spaniards to serve as laborers and paid with much-needed food (Hammond and Rey 1953:653). The proportion of non-local artifacts here was very small in comparison to numbers of local artifacts. Moreover we found no architectural modifications here, no window openings at all and no doorways with the dubious exception of one which, if it ever was a doorway, had been filled.

But somewhere in this big pueblo there would have been a center with the church, the convent occupied by the friars, and the cluster of houses modified to the needs of Oñate and his captains. There also would have been housing for some 42-50 families of lesser status each comprised of a colonist, his wife, and in some cases sons and daughters. (Hammond and Rey 1953:651). Families as such, one supposes, would not have been quartered in the West Mound barracks.

Our one clear reference to the church of San Miguel, their only permanent religious structure and quite certainly the only building in San Gabriel large enough to house a congregation of any sort, relates to the assemblage of September 7, 1601. Oñate and his party had not yet returned from their excursion out onto the Plains. The colonists were called together for mass apparently in this building. After mass the friars and the captains who together formed the core of the contriving dissident group dissatisfied with food shortage (second year of extreme drought), Oñate's rules against pillaging the natives, and the only minor successes in achieving conversions, spoke in turn, urging definite arrangements for desertion of the colony before its leader should return.

But where was that church?

On October 2 of the same year and in the same church, the 23 loyal soldier colonists who wanted to remain in New Mexico with their leader convened to record their group opinion of the lands and opportunities here, a paper intended for "his majesty or the viceroy of New Spain" (Hammond and Rey 1953:701-739).

The conflicting reports make it fairly evident that both sides were stretching some points in their own favor. But at this stage, without question, the psychology of the Spanish majority still was that of conquerors who expected to be supported and enriched by native peoples. Only a few of the colonists were appreciative of fresh land on which to make a living through hard labor.

We should add to this the old concept prevalent in Spain that none but people of very low class actually engaged in farming. Men who lived by cattle or sheep were of higher social position. Those who aspired to some-thing still better became soldiers or adventurers — and were supported.

But - back to our own immediate problems. *Where* had they placed their church? And where were those houses, so precipitously abandoned by the angry deserters that they might (we could hope) be expected to show some residue of some interesting trash left inside?

NOTE:
1. All Walls are of stone based contruction except where noted.
2. Heavy lines and roman numerals indicate size and number of Apartments.
3. Capital letters indicate separate rooms and areas.

LEGEND
- ⓜ Micaceous Bowl
- ◀ Post Hole
- ● Firepit
- ⏝ Metate
- ⊡ Stone Table
- ⊔ Metate Bin
- ˣ Indian Burial

Scale 1" = approx. 19'

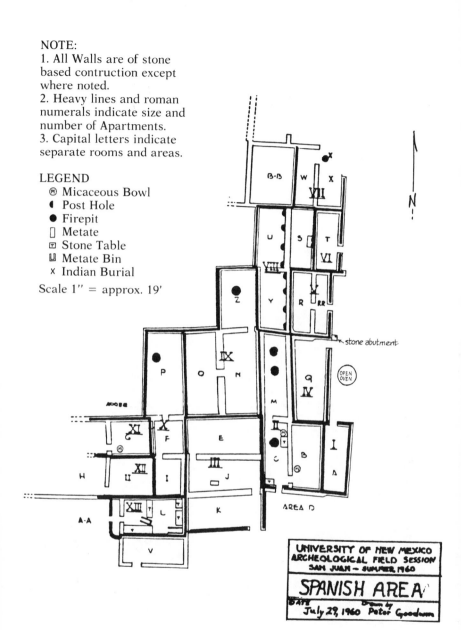

*Plan of Yungue Spanish Area*

43

*Panorama of Yungue site*

*Corner of Church foundation*

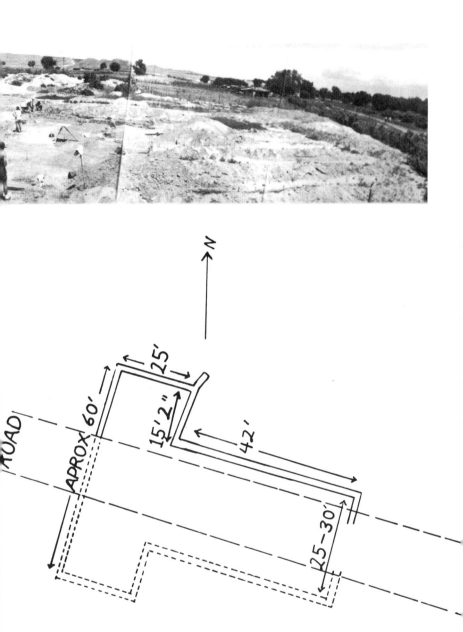

*The San Miguel Church at San Gabriel del Yungue*

*Links of Chain Mail found in Yungue*

*Candlestick base*

# The Spanish Center of San Gabriel: Apartments,* Kitchens, Domed Ovens, and The Permanent Church**

On June 28, 1960, with the midsummer sun blazing and temperature somewhere over 100, I stood on top of the upper East Mound, pushed my hat back to mop my forehead, and recalled the unhappy description of northern New Mexico by one of the sixteenth century Spaniards:

> ... eight months of summer and four of hell.
>
> (Hammond and Rey 1953:656)

Then something caught my attention. Immediately to the south of the lower end of that East Mound slope, the flat field was purple-blue with a great patch of wild morning glories. More than one archaeologist has observed that areas which chance to have profited from carbonaceous infiltration stemming from past occupation sometimes show plant growth appreciably more abundant or otherwise different from that common to the vicinity. So ---

Was it worth a try? Three of my students were just completing their east mound rooms. I sent them down to the morning glory patch to open two test trenches.

The first pit sunk uncovered a heap of large river cobbles which a little more digging proved to be the corner of a room, and, to the accompaniment of shouts and shrieks, two thirds of a late glaze decorated ware black-on-red bowl, broken into several sherds, were dusted off at floor-level. Following the cobbles, the delighted excavator traced the outline of the structure we came to designate (a few days later when newly visible outlines permitted mapping) as room E.

On the third day, the other trench, entering the 35 foot circular bed of morning glory blooms from the south, encountered an east-west wall 12

---

* Here we are capitalizing "Apartment" to indicate the importance of the Spanish concept in their reconstruction of the old Pueblo rooms into a new type of unit, appreciably more elaborate in some instances than the late prehistoric Pueblo apartments, the most obvious contrast being in the grace of floor doorways and cooking arrangements, though not seen in all.

** All rooms excavated were measured but we have here included the dimensions only for what seemed to have been the most important.

inches below present surface. At a depth of 2 inches below that surface, the ground was so hard that we were compelled to use pick and shovel. "Of course," said Mr. Montoya. This formerly had been a part of his corn field and for years was irrigated. The clay in the soil had solidified. But when an unlucky stroke dislodged several cobbles from the 3 stone wide, 1 stone high wall base, the excavators hastily reverted to troweling, and room A took shape. Long and narrow it was, with somewhat uneven walls (east 13'8", west 13'5", south 5'7", north 6'2"; wall thickness varied from 10" to 12"). A ground level doorway 2'5" wide, with stone sill, opened from the northwest corner onto the plaza, only a few feet from where we later were to uncover the tumbled remains of one of the Spanish domed ovens. (See description under house Q, Apartment IV.) Extra stones piled outside the northeast and southeast corners seemed to have provided small buttresses to the house. A wall, two fragments of corroded metal and a broken stone axe were found inside the room near the east wall.

Sunken below floor-level inside the west wall, a little less than one third of the room length from the southwest corner, was a complete, though broken, Biscuit B (Bandelier B/w) jar, its position suggesting customary Pueblo use as a storage container for food stuff such as ground cornmeal shortly to be used in cooking. We found no clear evidence, however, of a firepit in this room and it is quite possible that in many Apartments meal preparation was done in second story rooms where smoke could escape more easily and that this first story room served merely for storage and entrance. That the room had been used by Indian occupants before it was taken over by the Spaniards was strongly suggested by the presence of two hard clay plastered floor-levels, the upper one 10 inches above the lower and quite possibly laid by the Indians as part of the renovation changes mentioned in Spanish reports. A total of six layers of clay floor plaster could be counted. On the basis of its door opening to the exterior, we, somewhat hesitantly at first, gave room A the honor of representing Apartment I. An Apartment in our definition, consisted of one or more ground floor rooms connected to each other and/or to an outside plaza by floor-level doorways. We would picture an Apartment as occupied by a man and his family or a man and his servants. Evidence points to actual living quarters usually being on the second floor.

## Apartment I:

Room A, as we came to know when the plaza on which it fronted was cleared, marked the southeast corner of the massed block of houses in what we had been referring to as the South Field but which we soon came to recognize as "the major Spanish center." Our students at first dubbed it "the morning glory patch" but soon were happily calling it "the daisy patch" or "the pansy patch." Whatever the terminology, we had indeed stumbled upon our major goal. Movement of the young excavators into the newly opened territory was nothing less than a land rush almost overlapping their assigned tasks on the upper East Mound.

## Apartment II:

Rooms B (5'6" x 5'8") and C (same length but slightly narrower) on the west side of room A opened into each other through a floor-level doorway near the south end of their mutual wall. Room C was connected to room M, just to the north of C, by a similar doorway. (See map.) Their floors of the Spanish period (earlier floors lay below) were at the same level as that of room A for the Spanish period. The stone foundation between C and M was lowered by the Spaniards in removal of one row of cobbles over the width of that opening, and those stones or others had been used to build up the two sides of the floor-level doorway newly cut through the old wall. Rooms B, C, and M, like A, were narrow but long on the north-south axis. A doorway in the south wall of room C opened into what we designated as Area D, a jog at the south end of the East Plaza. This opening was interesting in that the stone foundation was high on the outer side of the wall but low on the inner side, which would indicate that one stepped down in entering the room. The plaza, thus, must have grown higher outside room C (and elsewhere) by deposition through time. I recall seeing some old Pueblo rooms in the 1930s, still occupied, into which one stepped down upon entering.

No question here: we had a three-room Apartment, with the probability of other living rooms "up ladder" on a second story. Unfortunately, in modern use of this land for cultivation, the remains of old roof fall had been so removed and distributed that all evidence from which we might have described upper stories was gone.

But there was even more reason for excitement. In the southwest corner near room C's outside doorway onto the plaza was a rectangle (2' x 2'6") paved with oval but flat river cobbles, and against the east wall toward the north end of the room was another similar area slightly larger in size and similarly paved except for some additions of broken flat rocks. "Floor tables!" The presence of ash and charcoal over the top of that east wall "floor table" immediately suggested its use as a hearth-griddle with upper surface an inch or so above floor-level. The stone paving would have assured its putting out extra heat and holding heat longer. It would have been something of a substitute for the ever popular Spanish brazier, still used in various forms in many lands. As a cooking device, although we could not know it until another week or two of work, it duplicated the four we were to uncover in our "kitchen center" (see discussion under Apartment XIII).

The "floor table" near the doorway in room C even could have been a "cobble hearth" (though we found no charcoal or ash associated with it), perhaps vented by a Spanish chimney hood. It is also possible that this "floor table" actually was used as a work base. Rural Spanish and Pueblo women of those days being without the legged tables we enjoy, had no choice but to become accustomed to kneeling at their work.

Just to the north of the innermost of these two cobble tables or hearths we found the restorable remains of a sooted micaceous culinary jar, once used for boiling but eventually as an on-the-spot storage container, probably for corn or wheat meal. Its base was sunken 10 inches below the floor-level of Spanish period. The top was approximately even with the floor and originally, to judge from old Pueblo custom, probably covered with a small sandstone slab.

On the opposite side of room C's doorway onto area D were the sherds of a broken Sankawi Black-on-cream bowl, evidence of Spanish use of contemporary Indian pottery as part of their household equipment.

An unplastered pit filled with charcoal and ash in room C apparently was the firepit used for other indoor cooking for Apartment II and possibly adjoining Apartment III during the Spanish period. The Spaniards may have placed some of their cobblestone table hearths to take advantage of already present roof smoke-hole-ladder-hatchways of Pueblo occupation days. In none of our excavations did we find evidence of any European type fireplace with chimney, though the settlers complained of bitter cold. The Indians, never having seen or used chimneys before Spanish contact, would have found building them most difficult, and apparently the Spaniards were not doing any major construction work themselves.

The one 10 inch deep unplastered circular depression as shown on our map for room M (north and south walls: 5'9", east and west walls: 17'10" and 17'9" respectively), the third first story room in this Apartment, could have served as a firepit into which pots would be set for boiling, but the other thought to have been a possible firepit may have been nothing more than a fire "spot" or "place" on the floor, conceivably to provide extra heat and light.

Apartment II certainly provides evidence that its first story rooms were planned for food preparation. A kitchen center in which the servants involved may have lived? Further equipment close at hand would have been the two domed ovens just outside, approximately on an imaginable line between areas KK and D (see later discussion). Those ovens could have served not only the two kitchen centers but other Apartments of this major Spanish center.

## Apartment III:

Apartment III, like II, was made up of three rooms, K, J, and E, renovated into an approximation of Spanish standards by putting in three floor-level doorways which connected the three large rooms and gave access to the outside area we refer to as KK, directly south of room K. The rooms of this Apartment were oriented on an east-west axis in contrast to the rooms of Apartments I and II and also to the other rooms farther northward. The 15 inch wall bases, wider than most, were of large cobbles. That unusual width possibly, but we have no way of being certain, may mark a reconstruction job by Indian workmen under direction of the Spaniards.

The walls of Apartment III, like their bases, were thicker than those of Apartments I and II, and some still showed patches of smooth mud plaster. The rooms also were wider (room E: north and south walls: 16' x 8', east and west walls: 8'0"; room J: north wall: 14'9", south wall: 15'1", east wall: 5'6", west wall: 6'3"; room K: north wall: 15'1", south wall: 15'10 1/2", east and west walls: 5'5"). Together they made up the largest Apartment we uncovered, and the artifacts found here are significant.

A Sankawi Black-on-cream bowl stood beside the doorway onto the plaza. The broken and incomplete Glaze F vessel found in the same room already has been noted, as well as part of a native griddle stone in room E. A broken Mexican-style 3-legged metate with only one leg intact lay on the floor of the middle room, J. Sherds in the fill, as in the other rooms of the Spanish area, showed a preponderant proportion of Biscuit A and Biscuit B, evidently still being used and possibly still being produced. Sankawi Black-on-cream and Potsuwi'i Incised, the next pair of successive types in the local time sequence, definitely were present, though in smaller proportions than the Biscuit ware.

Micaceous smeared indented and Micaceous washboard, locally made, were the two closely related and popular culinary wares present.

## Apartment IV

Apartment IV consisted of a single room, Q, adjoining room B on its north end. Like its neighbor, room A, it was long north-south (north wall: 6'10", south wall: 6'2", east wall: 15'6", west wall: 15'6"). The walls were 24 inches thick, twice the width of most other walls. A doorway onto the plaza had been put through at the northeast corner. The outside domed oven mentioned in discussion of room A was only 18 inches from room Q's east wall and quite certainly would have been used by the occupants of both rooms. That room Q, as we have suggested for room A and other rooms, had associated upstairs quarters to provide additional space or, most probably, the main living area, seems most likely. The ground floor-level, representing Spanish period use, was 6 inches above the original Indian floor-level. We located no features incorporated into either floor. The only two artifacts found were a pebble axe on the Spanish period floor and a floor polisher in fill 2 inches above the earlier and lower floor. Sherds from the fill duplicated the complex retrieved from all the other Apartments.

## Apartment V:

Apartment V, adjoining Apartment IV on the north, had two rooms, R and RR, though their combined width was no more than that across the north end of Apartment IV. The total length of the contiguous rooms R and RR, was 11'6"; room R varied from 4'9" to 4'11" in width, and room RR from 2'4" to 2'5". A doorway at midpoint in their common wall connected these two rooms. Another doorway opening through the center of the east wall of RR led into the plaza. A small test pit showed that RR's floor had been replastered three times. Room R showed no floor features, but in room RR what appeared to have been an unplastered firepit 7 inches deep, approximately 1 foot across and 3 feet long, well may have been used for cooking and heating. As some of the ash extended over the stub of the east wall, the possibility that this pit was intrusive must be recognized, but our opinion is that this scattering of ash resulted from the bulldozer activity which so unfortunately cut off all but the bases of walls throughout this central area of Spanish occupation. A few charred animal bones and a fragment from a broken metate lay in the ash. An obsidian scraper was found on the sill of the doorway between the two rooms. Sherds were more plentiful in the fill than in that of most rooms; the pottery complex was as found elsewhere in this site.

## Apartment VI:

Apartment VI, just north of the outer room of Apartment V, though its east wall extended a little farther into the plaza than that of V, had but a single ground floor room, T. Like the two rooms of Apartment V, T was long and narrow (north wall: 3'11", south wall: 3'2", east wall: 11'2", west wall: 11'4"). Its only special feature was the floor-level doorway south of center in the east wall, opening onto the plaza. Such long narrow rooms would have served well for storage of such necessities as corn and wood, which could have been racked up against the wall, but they also could have housed one man and a moderate amount of his equipment.

## Apartment VII:

Apartment VII had two rooms, W (north wall: 3'2 1/2", south wall: 2'10", east wall: 10'10", west wall: 11'0") and X (north wall: missing, south wall: 4'7", east wall: 6'0", west wall: 11'3"), connected by a doorway with a large cobble on one side at the north end of their mutual wall. The northern portion of the east wall of X as well as all of its north wall had been cut away after the period of Spanish occupation in making an intrusive Indian interment beneath floor-level. A crushed Sankawi Black-on-cream bowl (A.D. 1500-1600) lay near the skull, but whether it had been buried with the body or merely left in the room when the Spaniards moved out is uncertain.

This Apartment with its two narrow first story rooms and probably others on the floor above could have been used for storage or by one or two Spanish officers or by a man and his servant for scanty living quarters. As each of the Apartments so far discussed for that eastern edge of the house block bordering the East Plaza had a door opening to the exterior, Apartment VII probably had a similar opening in the north section now missing from the east wall of room X.

## Apartment VIII:

The outlining of Apartment VIII is difficult. Next to room T (Apartment VI) on the west, was an inner room S (north wall: 3'11", south wall: 4'3", east wall: 11'8", west wall: 11'1"), where a Pueblo type metate had been left standing against the east wall. There were no floor features. Neither the foundation stones of the west wall of room T or those of room U, adjoining S on the west side, showed any sign of a doorway into room S. As we know from work on other ruins and especially the closely related and contemporaneous great pueblo of Sapawe* only 30 miles distant, the Pueblo people often planned inner rooms for storage use and must have relied on a burning torch for any activity inside such rooms. Instead of being entered by a ladder from a hatchway in the roof, some were reached by means of a small doorway (usually closed by a stone slab) through which the owners crawled at 2 or even 3 feet above floor-level. No evidence of such a raised opening would have been preserved in the bulldozed area of Spanish occupation in San Gabriel del Yungue Ouinge.

Was room S alone or part of Apartment VIII, which included rooms U and V? Room S showed three successively laid floors at 8 inches, 14 inches, and 18 inches below present ground surface at the north wall, though the upper two had been broken by a late large intrusive pit containing black ash, charcoal, adobe, and quantities of what appeared to have been vegetable matter. This excavation, of course, could have destroyed evidence of a fire pit if one had been present. All we can safely say is that

---

\*     Pronounced Sa-pá-we.

the uppermost of the three first story floors must have been used by the Spaniards during their few years in this pueblo, for lying on that floor in the south end of room S was one of the most important artifacts retrieved.

This was identified by E. Boyd of the Museum of New Mexico as a small but exceptionally fine example of a sixteenth century gilded bronze religious medal, only about 1 inch in length. On one side was a relief showing the Trinity as frequently depicted in that period of the late Renaissance, though not today. God is seated with knees spread and a dove above his head; propped between his knees is the representation of a cross holding the crucified Christ. (Fig. 2) On the opposite surface of this medal we see St. Jerome kneeling in the desert, beating his breast with a stone. The symbolic lion lies at his feet. Boyd calls our attention to:

> possible authors of the Yunque relief of St. Jerome ... Jeronimo Fernandez of Avila, admired for his delicate handling of panels in low relief and Diego Siloe, the son of a famous Gothic style sculptor, Gil de Siloe. Diego had gone to Naples to execute a royal commission there and returned to his native Burgos by 1519. His work is in many Spanish churches, including several under the patronage of St. Jerome. He died in 1563. Juan de Ancheta, a Basque, had also been to Italy and executed altar pieces at Valladolid and Burgos. His working dates are 1566 - 1592.
>
> Religious medals found at other southwestern sites have been either those of poor quality which were distributed from Rome for distribution to pilgrims of foreign missions, or those struck in Mexico in the 18th century or more recently. Because of its high quality of artistic workmanship and even of the bronze alloy, and of its distinctly 16th century Spanish style, the Yunque medal is at present unique in its class.
>
> (E. Boyd 1961)

Three inches from the medal lay a half inch fragment of worked sea shell evidently brought by someone for trade, and in the southwest corner of the room a mano. A stone axe or hoe, a hammerstone, and a pottery polishing stone also were recovered from the same level as the metate and the medal. The sherd complex for this room was unusual only in the number of pieces present from micaceous culinary vessels which may have been stored here.

One can summarize our interpretation of room S by saying that it may have been used for storage by its original Indian owners and later taken over by the Spaniards for the same purpose. Certainly those newcomers would have had masses of goods to store, as we know from the inventories recorded at the times of inspection just before the two successive parties came up from Mexico. Numerous rooms the size of S would have been required for this, at least early in the history of this colony. But the quality of our medal strongly suggests that it is more likely to have been the personal possession of a churchman or a captain rather than lost from stored goods intended for trade to natives. It is not difficult to sympathize with that official, though we cannot call his name, who after going down to the first floor to check diminishing stores or hunt out something he needed, hurried back up the ladder, doused his blazing torch with relief — and later discover that his treasured medal, worn since leaving Spain, had broken from its chain and disappeared forever - or at least until we uncovered it in 1962.

We can definitely define Apartment VIII (rooms Y and U, with floor only 14" below present top of wall stubs) just west of Apartments V and VI, as a two room living arrangement, unless room S also belonged to it. The east wall of room U (north and south walls: 6'11", east and west walls: 10'5") was the west wall of room S, which matched room U in size. That mutual wall (16 inches in diameter), was somewhat thicker than most of the room walls, but apparently had not been considered strong enough to safely uphold a ceiling beam (viga) which had rested on or against it. Hence, at the base of that east wall in room U, as we deduced from four equally spaced little half circles of stone which once outlined their bases, four ceiling support posts had been set directly against the clay wall. The remains of one of those support posts still remained in its socket. A shallow unlined fire pit was located in the center of this room.

Room Y (north wall: 6'1", south wall: 5'4", east wall: 11'6", west wall: 10'11") adjoining U at the south end of the latter and with a floor-level doorway in its southwest corner, showed a duplicate set of four equally spaced stone-outlined half circles, evidently for the same purpose.

This was, indeed, an inner Apartment, two rooms without door openings separating it from the east plaza and a total of six rooms plus a possible very narrow storeroom between it and the central plaza on the west. Rooms Y and U certainly had been utilized; this was clear from the added post supports and the floor-level doorway. But how did anyone enter this apartment?

The only possibility would have been via a ladder reaching down through a hatchway in the roof. This is one of our best pieces of evidence that above these first story rooms there had been a second story complex supported by the walls of the first story and hence quite certainly duplicating in size and distribution the first story rooms. The same argument must apply to all the rooms between our Apartment VIII (rooms Y and U on the ground floor with second story rooms above them) and the central plaza west of this house block. In other words, all of those first story rooms with no indication of and no apparent possibility of entrance from the outside must have been entered via ladder from the second story. We must picture a set-back arrangement of second story rooms as described in various accounts of early Spanish explorers in our southwestern Pueblo territory and as is seen even today in Taos and Acoma Pueblos in New Mexico and Hopi in northern Arizona.

It really is not surprising that we found no evidence of firepits in rooms U and Y if the living quarters were on the floor above. The same must be surmised for most of the first story rooms in which no firepits were located. Remember that chimneys were unknown to the Pueblos. Smoke, being hot, rose and escaped through a roof hatchway usually used also for the entrance and exit of human beings by ladder. Smoke could have escaped from first story rooms only where these rooms extended out beyond those of the second story. This is the basic principle of the set-back or tiered arrangement characteristic of the late prehistoric Pueblo "Apartment houses" or "condominiums."

Following this line of reasoning, we can with some certainty make the general statement that most of the first story rooms in this massive house block of Yungue originally must have been intended for storage. They would have been as dark as any unlit basement. It was where exterior first story rooms stood out beyond those of the second floor, or where second floor rooms conceivably were removed from above first story rooms, that occupation of first floor rooms became practical. The Spaniards saw a point to the modification of those rooms by cutting ground level doorways through old walls. How many of the second story rooms were similarly modified we cannot know. The pre-Spanish Pueblo people themselves fairly frequently had connected upper story and sometimes bottom story rooms into Apartments by means of interior doorways but very rarely had they breached security by constructing ground floor doorways onto plazas or the outer world.

## Apartment IX:

With this explanation in mind, we come to examination of large inside Apartment IX, three connected rooms, Z, O, and N. Room Z (north and south walls: 6'4", east and west walls: 12'6") was of moderate size and as a firepit was found, somewhat north of center, we can be fairly sure that there was no room directly above it. First story Z must have been used for occupation or food preparation. In its southeast corner, room Z had a doorway into room N (north wall: 5'10", south wall: 6'4", east wall: 15'9", west wall: 15'5"), much larger than Z. N, in turn, had a doorway with a small step-down midway in the wall which separated it from room O (north wall: 6'5", south wall: 6'8", east wall: 15'6", west wall: 15'7"), very similar in size to N. Rooms N and O, without firepits, may have been used for storage or, less likely, living quarters, though they would have been very dark and chill even in summer. Nothing but the remnants of two possibly restorable vessels, one of Biscuit B and one of Micaceous ribbed culinary, were found in room O. In the fill of room N, between present surface and 5 inches above floor, lay two small bone whistles and an early iron nail. These may have fallen from above or been moved by the farmers bulldozer.

## Apartments X, XI, XII, and XIII: The Convent?

Inner Apartment X also was of three rooms, the large room P (north wall: 6'2", south wall: 7'8", east wall: 15'7", west wall: 15'4") just west of room O, small room F (north wall: 5'5", south wall: 5'8", east and west walls: 6'7") immediately to the south, and second small room I (north wall: 5'5", south wall: 4'4", east wall: 6'7", west wall: 7'4"). Each of these was connected to the other by a floor-level doorway.

No features were found in these rooms except for the unplastered roughly circular firepit (18" x 20" across and 18" deep) located in the northeastern sector of room P and largely filled with chunks of adobe when found. Some of those may have come from falling walls but others definitely had been part of the roof, as one knew from the parallel indentations of reeds used to line the ceiling. This debris, which had collected in the pit as the house decayed, held a number of interesting objects, most of which fell from the story above, along with the roof debris. At only 3" below floor level a horseshoe-shaped piece of metal (not an actual horseshoe) was found and just below it a fragment of Spanish handblown glass, wine glass or tumbler, in which bubbles provided decoration. Between 7 and 14 inches down, a fragment of copper appeared, as well as a pumpkin seed, a bone awl, and a little obsidian flake saw (1/2" x 1 3/4" x 1 1/7"), native Pueblo items. Two small smooth stones conceivably used in polishing pottery lay in the bottom 2 inches of firepit fill. Sherds scattered throughout that fill were of the mixed pottery complex found everywhere in our excavations of San Gabriel del Yungue.

In 1960, Apartment XI had appeared to consist of small room G, directly west of F, apparently connected by a doorway to our then partly excavated room GG at its west end. (Doorway openings, by oversight, unfortunately were not always indicated on the 1962 map Fig. 5.) At that time Apartment XII looked to be a duplicate of XI, with "room H," actually the lower half of long room GG-H, appearing to be the large room into which room II opened. The 1962 excavations seemed to indicate that GG and H were only the two ends of a single long room, though the floor was 3 inches higher at one end than at the other. Room GG-H appeared to have been connected to room FF by a floor-level doorway. This apparently left room

G and H, just south of it, as possibly individual separate rooms. Today we cannot be certain in unraveling this problem of "Apartments XI and XII." We are inclined to favor the 1960 interpretation of room G having been connected to room GG by a doorway, the reconstruction which would give Apartment XI a level floor. Room H appeared to have been connected by a doorway to room H, the two making up Apartment XII. But being certain of doorway openings in some of these low wall remains was very difficult.

On the floors of these rooms were numerous fragments of metal and chunks of volcanic tuff which we soon were to discover matched those in area AA. Nothing of this sort had been found in our walls or on floors or plazas before. What? What? We were on the edge of our most important discovery, but first we must unwrap our second most important, "the kitchen center," probably the focal point of San Gabriel's Franciscan monastery, the first in New Mexico.

Apartment XIII clearly put together by the Spaniards as a room for meal preparation on more than a family scale, was by far the most interesting of any we excavated. Comprised of the two parts of room L, plus a small antichamber later added (for storage?) at the western entrance (see 1960 map, Fig. 7), it had been constructed as a single long room (north wall: 11'5 1/2", south wall: 12'1/2", east wall: 5'10", west wall: 6'2") similar to any of the three rooms of adjoining Apartment III. Room V and possibly even open area VV, just beyond the south wall of V also were a part of this same "Apartment" or complex.

The remaining walls of room L varied from 7" to 20" in height, as in so many of the rooms and higher than in some. There was evidence of two floors, one at 16" and one at 20" below present surface. That deeper and earlier floor ran *beneath* the floor features, whereas the later floor, apparently laid in the Spanish take-over when the features were built, *curved up to* their edges. The doorway in the west wall led into a small storeroom (6'6" x 2'1 1/2") added during reconstruction. Its floor was 3 inches higher than that of room L itself, the storeroom floor being at the level which the plaza outside had gained by accretion through the three centuries the house block had stood before the Spanish influx. As can be seen from the 1960 map, the west wall of that little storeroom, with its doorway onto the plaza, had a curved corner whether by accident or the intent to provide a convenient location for a storage jar. The curved area had only a series of single cobblestones as its base, though the main west wall of this storage room had the usual 2-cobblestones-wide foundation.

The reason for our great interest in Apartment XIII stems from the features found still in place and not duplicated elsewhere.

First -- the "tables." We already have noted two low "cobblestone tables" which could have been used for preparation of foods, or as a base on which to built a fire, against two walls in room C of Apartment II. Here, in room L, cobblestone "table #1" extended east-west along the interior wall for 5'7" from the southwest corner. It was a slab only a few inches above floor level but 18 inches wide, formed, like those in C, by laying two rows of large cobblestones or three rows of similar stones in rows, filling in with smaller smooth stones, and using adobe mortar to hold them in place. Neither this table nor the others appear to have been joined to the walls; they are separated by 3 or 4 inches of space but it is conceivable that this once was filled in with mud plaster. Directly opposite the end of "table #1," was "table #2," only slightly over 1 foot in width, extending southward 3 feet from the north wall and actually providing a divider for the room.

Two more "tables" were found in the east end of room L, one in the corner, attached to the north wall, measuring only 12" x 8" and the other, seven inches to the south, measuring 2'5" x 8". It is possible (though unlikely) that they had been the two parts to one "table," as no cobbles were found in the interval between them.

Then - just to the south of this second of the two north-south "tables," actually wedged between one table and the south wall of the room, was a metate bin, something we found nowhere else in our excavations at this site. It had been made of large cobble stones set on edge, adobe, as usual, being used for mortar between the stones. A large Pueblo style metate was set into the bin so that it sloped toward the east wall. The woman who did the grinding would have been on her knees, crushing the corn or wheat with her mano or handstone, much as some of us used to scrub our clothes on a washboard. A second metate bin had been built at an angle between the ends of "tables" 1 and 2, a large stone being used at the east upper end to assure the slope. Smaller stones were used in building up the sides. A second large local style Pueblo metate still was in place there. (See our 1960 map in which these details show more clearly than on the 1962 map.)

And who would the users of these four low tables and the metates have been? Clearly, room L was a kitchen center set up for grinding and indoor cooking. As the metates were of the blocky Pueblo style rather than of the three-legged Mexican type, it is possible that the users were Pueblo women, hired for the duty, though setting those metates so much higher than in native homes and not in the usual aligned sequence of two or three in a single bin suggests that the users were not Pueblo persons. Servants from Mexico?

A most likely hypothesis is that one or more of these low cobblestone "tables" could have served as a base on which to build a fire above which, supported by four stones, one of the thin slab Pueblo stone griddles or the Spanish iron or copper griddles could have been set up to bake corn or wheat tortillas (somewhat limp unleavened thin cakes, the major breadstuff of Mexico), on the surface. The low bench-form fire base set against a wall of the cooking room and vented by a long hood which caught the smoke to carry it up through one, two, or three roof chimneys (depending on length of bench base, which might take up one full wall) was introduced to the Pueblos by the Spaniards. It is shown in many early photographs of Hopi, Zuni, and some of the Rio Grande Pueblos. A few cooking rooms of this type still are kept up by the more conservative of the Rio Grande Pueblos, such as Santo Domingo and Zia, for preparation of meals, old style, at the time of meetings of various of their religious secret societies. This long fire bench, if one might call it that, also served as location for fires over which one cooked stews of meat and whatever vegetables were at hand. The cooking vessel, whether of Indian pottery or Spanish metal, was held upright merely by being well settled in the embers or balanced by a few "fire dog" stones (field stones selected for size and shape) or the very convenient metal Spanish tinamaeste,[*] as still termed in northern New Mexico. This last consisted of a flat hollow circle of iron, supported by three legs and moved by means of a straight projecting handle, commonly with a decorative twist at its outer end.[**]

The kitchen room, L, also appears to have had one actual firepit (unless it was a pit for temporary disposal of ashes) near the edge of the stone "table" in the northeast corner of the room. Nearby, set 10 inches into the floor, with its top at floor level, was a sooted jar of culinary ware. Such containers, old pieces of pottery frequently being used thus by Pueblos, would have held corn meal for immediate use in cooking.

Our guess is that this kitchen center pertained to the five adjoining rooms, P, F, G, I, and II (Apartments X, XI, and XII) which well could have been occupied by the local clergy as a convent complex. Actual living quarters presumably would have been on the second story, as all of these on ground floor were inner rooms without access to any light or ventilation. The ground floor presumably would have served for storage, except for room P where a firepit was reported.

We would add one other room, V, directly adjoining room L on the south, to our kitchen Apartment XIII. This room caught our attention as being peculiar in having abundant stone in its east and south wall bases but

---

[*]  Pronounced Tína-mice-te.

[**]  The Pueblo griddles of today are of metal or of stone of various grades of smoothness achieved in the past through careful polish, a topping of fine clay plaster, and a final finish of tallow rubbed into the heated surface. The degree of fineness of surface was varied in relation to the type of corn cakes or "native paper bread" it was to be used for. As no such griddles have been made for many years, the old ones handed down in a family are carefully cherished.

far less in the bases of the other two walls. One begins to wonder whether those and some of the other old walls were not removed and replaced under Spanish direction because they were faulty at the time of take-over. We found a few bases of old walls extending out from some part of the main houseblock but seeming not to lead anywhere and obviously not a part of the Spanish period complex. When old Yunque was appropriated by Oñate to be repaired in part, as well as redesigned into something approaching the Spaniards' concept of what a town should be, there certainly would have been some ruined structures to re-do or remove.

A wide floor-level opening (not shown on 1960 map but present on map of 1962) was cut into the south wall of room V near its southwestern corner. Complete lack of floor features suggests possible use of the room for storage of staples used in the daily food preparation in grinding-cooking complex L. However, room V could have been utilized for other preparation of food than that in specialized workroom L or even quite conceivably as a dining chamber for the Franciscan group.

Just beyond room V's only wall still showing good definition, that on its south side, was what appeared to have been an open space, area VV. It may have been roofed as a portal or shade at one time. If VV ever was an entire room, that would have been some time earlier, with all walls except one shared with room V lost. The adjoining space to the east, directly south of room K, was a similar type of area, possibly once a room or a roofed portal, which we designated as KK. Both of these spaces or "areas" appear to have had no floor other than the original ground surface which came to be covered with a series of ash lenses, adding up to some 14 inches of depth in VV. At between 10 and 14 inches below present surface, these lenses held a heavy accumulation of iron and copper fragments, from nails to flat chunks. There also were bits of juniper wood, probably from roofing of V and/or VV, adobe chunks from roof or wall, animal bones, a considerable number of sherds, a section from a broken sandstone griddle, and even eggshells. There obviously had been no town clean up squad.

Among these items at a depth of 18 inches and a full 59 inches south of the wall shared by area VV with room V lay the exfoliating half of what once had been the base of an opalescent hand-blown stemmed wine glass made either in Spain or representing the Cadiz glass of north Africa. A bent, heavy, and corroded iron spike or nail was found at a depth of 17 inches, only a few inches northwest of the glass fragment.

The simple cooking facilities of the Spaniards as we found them at San Gabriel parallel those used by some Pueblo families into the present century. Their one other major need would have been ovens in which to bake the raised wheat bread so dear to Spanish taste and shortly to that of the Pueblo people, as well. The leavening of that bread? Presumably the powdered burned limestone (baking powder) still being prepared and used by some Pueblo families up into the 1930s. The Spanish oven was modeled on the old domed outdoor type still used in north Africa, rural Spain, in the seventeenth century in England and doubtless in other countries. It spread through Latin America and our Southwest, from Spaniards to Pueblos, to the Navajo, with small variations, and it was used through New England and elsewhere on our east coast after being introduced by the colonists from Great Britain. I have found such an oven fine for roasting meat, and my Pueblo friends still cherish theirs for baking bread, pies, and cookies for the many religious feast days.

The first domed ovens of which we have evidence in our Southwest are the five examples our field crews uncovered along the southwestern corner of the "main Spanish section" of San Gabriel. We previously noted the base of a domed oven close to the ground-level doorways of rooms A and Q opening onto the east plaza (see 1960 map Fig. 5). What we actually found were the stones which once composed the base for each such oven, those stones still forming an approximately circular clump. The individual cobbles averaged 3 to 5 inches thick and the clump extended from 45 to 57 inches in diameter. The main portion, the dome, probably was built up from the stone platform by the Pueblo wall-building technique of coursed adobe. The oven base or floor, consisting of these stones held together by adobe mortar, would have stood 6 inches or less in height. The domed oven rising from the base probably stood 3-4 feet high. An arched opening was made at the bottom front of the dome, just above the floor so that wood could be inserted for the fire. A circular opening a few inches across would have been left in the upper dome to provide a draft.

After a few hours of heating the oven, the embers and ash could be quickly swept out with a broom of leafy brush (today with a wet rag on the end of a stick), the food inserted, and the door opening closed with a piece of metal, if available, or a soaked mat or leafy short branches.

In time the dome would melt away, yes, if not periodically repaired, but the stones would be left unless removed by later occupants of the site or by their bulldozers. Two of our oven remains were still humped when found.

The space adjoining room V and that immediately to the east and hence directly south of room K (the southern room of big Apartment III) we designated area KK. Like area VV it appeared to have had no walls and no floor other than the original ground surface onto which room K opened with a neat floor level doorway which had been cut into its southeast corner. Like area VV, area KK had been a portion of the plaza close enough to the house block to have accumulated ash, sherds, and general debris, including a great number of fragments of worn-out metal components of unidentifiable Spanish equipment (see map of metal finds) and also a great number of animal bones (Mindeleff, V. 1897:162-167; Underhill 1946:92-85) possible evidence that butchering as well as baking may have taken place here.

These two domed ovens actually would have been no more than a few feet from the entrances to room C of Apartment I and room K of Apartment III. They could have been used in baking for the two units inhabiting those apartments. They also, however, were close enough to rooms L and V of the "kitchen center" (Apartment XIII) to have been used as part of their culinary equipment, as well. One of those ovens was found ringed on three sides by an ash deposit four inches deep and thick with potsherds, especially those of the local micaceous culinary ware. Our explanation would be that the pottery may or may not have indicated common use of such vessels in the ovens but that Spaniards certainly were not meticulous about carrying kitchen trash to any distant site for deposition. The ash may have been brushed from the oven, as is done today by the Pueblos, and left at its edge. Thus, covered bowls of food such as *panocha*, the old fashioned but still greatly appreciated Pueblo sprouted wheat sweet pudding, its recipe as well as the wheat coming from Spanish contact, could be buried in warm ashes to bake slowly while the heat remained. Today this ash often is confined in an enclosure outlined by a curved clay wall only a few inches high at one side of the oven entrance, and it is quite possible that the low unburned clay wall which appeared to have extended out from the side of one of our pair of ovens may have been designed for that purpose.

The three other clumps of cobbles similar to the bases of our other domed ovens all were uncovered in excavation of the east plaza itself. It seems probable that still others would be found in the main plaza, in front of the Spanish Apartments facing onto it, could that land be excavated.

## Area AA:

Other students were moving westward at plaza level, following the northern edge of area AA (west of room L, Apartment XIII, the "kitchen center") in hopes of locating the southwestern corner of our big houseblock. Its western limit necessarily defines the eastern edge of the central plaza at the time of Spanish take-over except, of course, for whatever may have been torn down, as hinted by the partially traceable portions of old walls we encountered.

Area AA could be generally described as an open passageway running westward from our kitchen center, to that old central plaza. But by making a jog to get around the possible storeroom or dining room associated with the kitchen center one also could walk eastward, passing big Apartment III and busy area D, near the southeast corner of the Spanish Apartment area, to emerge in the southeastern corner of the east plaza. This passageway would have been a somewhat irregular and narrow street, passable on foot or horseback.

We quickly discovered, in the Spanish period there had been only one apartment between the southwestern corner of our houseblock and room L, though two projecting remnants of earlier period were encountered. That single corner apartment was notable in possibly having been made up of two long slender rooms, FF and GG-H, on a north-south axis, with a doorway connecting the two at the south end of their dividing wall. At least this apparently had been the original plan (see 1962 map), though there was some evidence that room GG-H in the Spanish period had been made into two small rooms (1960 map), the floor of its north end, GG, being 3 inches different in level from that of H, the southern end of that room. A Spanish floor level door way led from GG into G, and a second one from H into II. To the north of these two associated rooms we outlined three more of similar proportions, two being distinguished by narrow "cubby holes" along the full length of the room on their plaza side. With no more than 12 to 16 inches of width, these may have been wall compartments for piñon nuts or other foods such as the Pueblo peoples characteristically hid away in preparation for the occasional dry years of near famine which they knew must be expected. That deposits in sealed wall cavities were not unusual we know from numerous references, but descriptions of such pockets are non-existent.

# The Church of San Miguel: First Permanent Spanish Church in our Southwest

The north edge of area AA, from west to east, consisted of the front walls of the rooms at the south edge of the main houseblock. This was relatively clear even if that front was not in a straight line.

Our group that had been concentrating its efforts on finding the south edge of this "area" and uncovering its center down to the old Spanish period level now found itself striking rocks and more rocks at 6 to 12 inches below present surface. The stones were not heavy; the material was volcanic tuff. But they were so numerous and in some spots so compacted that at times one had the impression of a fallen wall. Fallen from where? Certainly not the rooms on the north side of AA. Their walls were of coursed adobe. The stones *looked* as if they had fallen from the south and spread as they struck the earth. Not only in open area AA but also scattered in the fill inside the rooms on the north edge of that area. This meant that those houses must have been abandoned and partly filled with debris from their fallen roofs before the volcanic tuff was strewn.

At 16 1/2 inches below the present surface of area AA we found a fragment of corroded iron. At a depth of 17 inches we encountered a lens of "greenish gray to reddish ash" in which there was a scattering of charcoal, more of the rocks, numerous fragments of corroded iron, small fragments of sea shells, and a few animal bones. At 27 inches, the soil changed to an orange color. Burned? A few feet farther to the west we ran into what appeared to be the remains of an early but now buried wall remnant across the top of which ran a newly uncovered and definitely existent wall of gray unshaped volcanic tuff chunks set in adobe mortar. Its total present height averaged approximately 14 to 18 inches. *What* had we discovered?

And who could have been constructing not the standard cobble-based coursed adobe wall but, instead, a stone wall, and within 10 feet of the "Spanish Apartment district?"

How could we guess that we were in the process of discovering San Gabriel's only permanent church, dedicated to San Miguel but "lost" probably at least since the late seventeenth century.

Burned and pulled down at the time of the Pueblo Rebellion of 1680, like some at other pueblos? Most likely, for Popé, the main leader of that rebellion, was a native of San Juan Pueblo and war chief of the tribe, though during his work of planning the revolt he moved his headquarters to Taos.

Adams and Chavez in their study, *The Missions of New Mexico, 1776*, note that:

> Alvarez tells us that a church was under construction [in San Juan Pueblo] in 1706 ..., and in this case it is probable that there was little, if anything, left of the pre-Revolt structure.                    (Adams and Chavez 1956:85, fn. 2)

One could hardly suppose that Popé would have left this first solidly built Spanish church standing, a major symbol of the Pueblos' problems which in 82 years had grown to the point of being unbearable.

It took us considerable following of walls, as well as thinking, before we could realize that the puzzling scatter of chunks of volcanic tuff in and around area AA and the adjoining houses originally had been a part of that church. It was *here* the group of Spanish dissidents had met to document and plan their desertion from Oñate's ranks while he still was out on the Plains. And, a few weeks later, it was *here* that Oñate's supporters had met to pen their admiration of the governor's good leadership, the rich productiveness of lands surrounding the colony, and their personal intent to remain in New Mexico, as originally planned.

But how did we really know this was the church so long visualized but so little actually sought by historians or anyone else?

At first we had little hint. Our students were following, in professional fashion, that first east-west wall of rough volcanic tuff blocks. At both its ends, a distance of but 25 feet, the wall turned a right angle corner to the south, heading for and then passing beyond the barbed wire fence at the edge of the access road which marked the limit of our permit area.

*But who could have there abandoned the only stone wall we had even glimpsed in our site?* Leaving that western north-south wall at the fence, we followed its eastern mate which, just beyond that fence, made another right angle corner. Here it dropped lower, beneath the surface of the drainage ditch bordering that access road. On we dug and faster. At 18 feet to the east of the right angle corner, we encountered a 6 foot gap which originally must have been space for a side doorway. The wall then continued eastward for 28 more feet, where it turned another right angle corner. Road grading had removed the corner itself, but by taking out a few shovelsful of soil toward the south edge of the little access road (at an hour when no traffic was expected) we immediately picked up about 2 feet of the short north-south wall (foundation) of what would have been the front of the old church of San Miguel. There was no question: we had one half the transept and one half the nave of a cruciform structure. The old church was split lengthwise down its center by today's little dirt roadway.

More we dared not do unless our permit were re-written, so we measured and plotted *one half the outline of the church of San Miguel*, (see drawing Fig. 8) the major find of our three seasons of work. Then we carefully re-covered those excavations to provide them what protection was possible. That evening, San Juan families in returning as usual to their homes south of the little road and on the West Mound, unwittingly drove up the nave of the oldest church in the United States with at least the lower section of its walls still intact.[*]

Our east-facing edifice would have been 67 feet long, with the nave 25-30 feet across (figures estimated in judging the center of transept from measurement of its clearly outlined northern half). That transept was 25 feet deep (east-west) and approximately 60 feet across (north-south). The south end of the transept, after running under the access road, would have extended some 5 feet onto land belonging to the Martinez family.

The construction material had been the gray volcanic tuff available within a few miles at the base of the Pajarito Plateau. Tuff is not difficult to cut, especially if one does not insist on neat rectangular blocks. The stone was light to transport, and adobe for mortar was at hand.

In the meantime, others of the students had been clearing the interior of the north transept. Some of the volcanic tuff wall stones lay strewn over its interior, as well as outside to the north, the walls having fallen or been pulled down after the roof was burned. A Spanish button of copper with raised design lay 13 inches below surface, 26 1/2 inches south of the inner side of the north wall. A fragment of copper or bronze lay 33 inches south of that north wall, and 96 inches west of the northeast corner, at a depth of 19 inches. At 25 inches down, ash was plentiful, as it had been outside in area AA. The contrast was in lack of sherds (understandably) in the church fill. When the church roof was burned, the ash would have collected on the eroded clay floor of that period, very likely in or shortly after 1680. It also had spread to the houses already ruined in the 70 years since total abandonment, on the northern edge of area AA.

At the same depth of 25 inches, 90 inches from the northeast corner of the transept and 27 inches south of the north wall, we encountered the

---

[*]   The first church at St. Augustine, Florida, was constructed of wood and thatch. The site is there, but nothing of that structure built in 1567, the Nombre de Dios Mission (Doctrina) is thought to remain. As explained earlier, the first church constructed by Oñate's colonists, completed sufficiently for use in September 1578, after two weeks of labor, probably was of jacal (upright posts and clay), which could not have been expected to last either. It was dedicated to Saint John the Baptist. The exact location remains unknown.

skeleton of a Pueblo male lying fully extended, his hands folded on his chest. The characteristic occipital flattening (in no way physically harmful) resulting from use of the baby board in his infancy, as well as the presence of shovel-shaped incisors (much more frequently found in persons of Indian blood than in others), convincingly indicated that he had not been Spanish. His acceptance of Christianity was indicated by a circular piece of bone with an incised cross on its surface having been laid on his torso. He well may have been the native sacristan or possibly some other native official aiding the Spanish churchmen.

A second extended native burial, similarly with hands folded on his chest, lay near him (see 1962 map). It is possible that the Spanish button already mentioned as conceivably worn as a pendant had been associated with that second burial.

No other interments were found in this transept or in what little we could dig of the nave.

With the church of San Miguel finally located, definitely in the area "near the Martinez house" as some of the San Juan men had suggested on the basis of old tradition, it certainly was where it should be at the opening of the plaza, as favored in early Spanish village planning. We immediately became re-convinced of the probability that our kitchen center and the adjoining rooms well could have been the convent. The north end of the church transept was only 10 feet from the west end of room L, our "kitchen center." The doorway opening from room V, the possible dining room or storeroom for said kitchen, was a little less than 20 feet from the big doorway opening in the north wall of the the transept. This would have been almost as convenient as if the convent had been attached to the church itself.

And, in the course of our uncovering areas VV and KK while clearing the "right of way" (area AA) from the main or central pueblo plaza to the east plaza, we chanced upon a special find we never could have predicted — what apparently were the two old altar candlesticks. One was uncovered by Gail Schroeder in troweling at a depth of 10 inches below the present ground surface of area KK, which would put it 4 inches above the floor level of adjoining room K and 81 inches south of the south wall of that room. The second candlestick was found by a chance flip of the trowel of John Speth (now Dr. John Speth, of the University of Michigan) at a depth of 16 inches from the surface and 21 1/2 inches south of the inside face of the south wall of room V. The two actually were only about 3 feet distant from each other, one inside a room and the other apparently outside.

The candlesticks were very similar to each other in size and pattern but not identical. They would have served very nicely as a pair gracing an altar. Their material was bronze, heavily corroded when uncovered but responding well to cleaning. Both measured approximately 4 inches high and 5 inches across the circular base[*] with some corrosion having eaten through. One or both had held a candle in an upward projecting cup, such as we usually see today, or instead, had held the candle impaled on a short spike. Both arrangements were used in the sixteenth century.

As to how these items came to be discarded where we found them, we can only make suggestions. They may have been left in the church during its mission period before the destruction which we have dated as probably close to 1680. The friars ever had been concerned at the chances of leaving the Indians without benefit of church after they had been persuaded to accept the faith, as the single churchman who did not leave San Gabriel with the other dissidents explained in the letter he sent with them to Mexico.

On the other hand, one might reason that the Spaniards in moving from San Gabriel to Santa Fe would have needed those candlesticks for their own new church. Counter to that are the repeated complaints of churchmen and secular leaders before that move: their equipment was inadequate and wearing out, as well as foodstuffs and all other goods running short.

It well could be that the new Governor, Peralta, arranged for some replacements of church as well as other equipment when he, himself, replaced Oñate.

So the candlesticks could have been tossed away by the Spaniards themselves. Or they could have been thrown out with some fury by the Pueblo revolutionists when they were destroying the church of San Miguel at the onset of the rebellion. We were more than happy to retrieve them!

## The East Plaza and Its Trenches

One of the hazards in analysis of this type of site was the known fact that for decades it had been plowed, disced, and bulldozed, removing all upper portions of walls, and stirring up everything between the surface and the plowline, 10 inches below. Irrigation of fields planted directly on top of the ruin had turned the adobe-laden soil to almost brick-like hardness. There also was the matter of several families having lived on top of the East Mound within this and the last century, as we learned from San Juan elders,

---

[*] The similarity of these candlesticks to one recovered from the Pine Log Creek Site (1Ba462), a protohistoric Indian burial mound in southwestern Alabama, is surprising. That burial mound is thought to have been associated, possibly, with an Indian village visited by Tristan de Luna in 1560. Remnants of other Spanish equipment, iron spikes, iron "half axe," muleshoe, and some of the badly corroded unidentifiable objects also are very reminiscent of our finds from Yungue. With only some 38 years difference in date, this would be expectable.

to some of whom we sent native Spanish-speaking students for interviews. Finally, our own archaeological group, working on rooms in the northern section of the East Mound during 1959 and 1960, had arranged for much of the fill they were removing to be pushed by a tractor over onto the East Plaza surface so that they might better reach the lower parts of walls. At that time none of us knew that an East Plaza ever had existed.

The Yungue East Plaza, as best we could tell, measured approximately 90 feet from the area of domed ovens at the edge of area KK northward to where the east-west rows of rooms seemed to shrink to no more than four across. Our 1962 investigation of that East Plaza work began with laying in a grid outlining a series of trenches to run parallel to each other, 10 feet apart, and at a right angle to their common base line. Our hope was to locate the vertical contours of the plaza floor as well as something of its stratigraphic profiles and periphery (see 1962 map). The trenches were to be excavated in 4 foot sections, 2 feet wide, and holding to successive levels 6 inches in depth after the upper relatively soft surface soil, 1 foot or slightly more in depth (which we, ourselves, had so unwisely added) had been discarded. The total depth supposedly would reach sterile bottom soil that, as we found, could be as much as 48 inches below present surface. Should the trench appear to offer nothing of interest, it could be either abandoned or pursued outside the original confines. All sherds and artifacts, Spanish or Indian, animal bones, and anything else that might appear to have importance were to be measured in for location.

The results of this exercise turned out to be far more rewarding than originally expected, and in various categories. Our initial intent to keep a trench narrow until we had discovered that its widening would or would not be worth while, was somewhat relaxed early in our procedure as it became obvious that heavy railroad picks would have to be used to break up the super-hard soil at the level where irrigation water had penetrated the field. That type of hand labor simply required more space for movement.

Our first general observation was that much of the northeastern portion of what we were considering plaza originally had been lower than most of the land nearby, perhaps as the result of early river channeling, and had been utilized for what students were inclined to call a "trash pit." With somewhat more experience in the customs of the Pueblo peoples, they would have recognized it as an "ash pile," to use the native term. The Pueblo way of life emphasizes communal neatness more than does that of modern America and certainly more than that of old Spain. An ash pile is not a trash pit nor a garbage heap, in our sense of those terms. It is a growing mound which consists primarily of the ash and floor sweepings cleaned out from the houses of an area and carried to the heap which belongs to that neighborhood. It may contain the remains of old baskets, pottery, and various household objects, as well as ash, and through the association of those objects with the ancestors, now gone, the entire heap assumes a semi-sacred aura. Offerings are placed upon it at times of religious affairs, and outsiders and in some cases even the villagers are not permitted to walk over the pile. Wet garbage, as we think of it, does not go into such heaps. A village in the past usually had more than one ash heap, the term referring not only to the presence of the ash from household fires but also to the revered and kindly Ash Boy, the major patron of households who is thought of as the younger of the two fire gods or spirits long important in Mexico and still so at Zuni and elsewhere in our native Southwest.

Archaeologists customarily look for ash piles near prehistoric sites in the hope that by careful study of their stratification, usually with successive types or complexes of pottery providing our major information, the chronological periods represented can be established.

In our case, work on the East Plaza study could not be completed because of time shortage. Workers never reached the east end of certain trenches and a few, laid out, were not dug at all. Our results, however, point to thorough and careful excavation and screening of material not only from trenches but covering that entire area as one of the most important projects still much needed and possible at San Gabriel del Yungue Ouinge.

The debris remaining in those trenches and between them should carry a great deal of information. In summarizing results of our own work there, our initial statement would refer to the discovery that the northeast corner of the plaza, had held an ash pile in Pueblo days from about A.D. 1250 or 1300 into the Spanish period. Its base was as far as 4 feet lower than the overall plaza floor. Some actually stratified areas marked by successive pottery types still may be present there, undisturbed, but most of the contents of such a pile have been, as in other parts of this pueblo, badly mixed by modern plowing, bulldozing, adobe-making, etc., though the pottery types as represented by sherds, even if not in original order, would indicate something of overall time of occupation and perhaps something of trade patterns.

Second, the Spaniards in their day used the native ash heap as a depository for their own household cleanings and general "trash." Such material should have been at a level above the Pueblo deposit, but as we said for the mixtures of what could have been time marker pottery types elsewhere, in San Gabriel, their positions had been changed through years of plowing and other field work, the early historic insertion of burials into older fill, and the later disturbance and re-interment of skeletal material during years of local land use.

Our trench excavations indicated that the East Plaza Spanish trash deposit did not extend farther than 30 feet east of our baseline and in the main formed a curved band only about 15 feet across. Its cultural content of sherds (Pueblo, Spanish imported crockery, and glass ware), beads, and metal will be discussed in relation to the total distribution of these artifacts as we retrieved them from the site of San Gabriel as a whole.

## The Overwhelming Distribution of Metal in San Gabriel

Our unexpectedly fairly prolific yield of iron, copper, and bronze fragments from San Gabriel presumably represents worn out bits from all the types of items listed in those inventories made before Oñate's party, including the supplemental group which left Mexico reaching San Gabriel in the winter of 1600-1601. The much lesser collection of Spanish items found relatively whole, corroded but recognizable for what they were, is a small treasure trove to the archaeologist-historian.

Of all the Spanish artifacts we uncovered, those of metal had by far the widest distribution, and those of iron were more than twice as numerous as those of copper, brass, and bronze, taken together. (See map Fig. 4 showing location of finds of metal in East Mound area.) All but a precious few, however, could be listed only as unidentifiable fragments. Through almost four centuries the rains of summer and the snows of winter at our altitude had subjected the metals to corrosion, a process unquestionably hastened after the irrigation ditch was installed and water put into the fields planted directly above the remaining old walls and cultural fill material. Most of our artifacts, fragmentary or not, were cleaned in the laboratory of the Maxwell Museum at the University of New Mexico Anthropology Department by Ted Frisbie (now Dr. Ted Frisbie of the University of Southern Illinois at Edwardsville), using the electrolyte process. This process cut down on the original size of many, and some became very fragile. When certain of them, their original core now gone, were found to simply disappear under such treatment, a few were selected for no more than mechanical cleaning, if any.

It was interesting to note that the rooms of the West Mound, the "barracks," yielded about as many items, including those in fairly good shape, as all of the big house block of the "main Spanish area." Although considerably more was found toward the south than the north end of that house block, metal objects and an occasional piece of crockery (Majolica ware) came to light as far north as Mr. Lee Montoya's fence, our working limits. The greatest concentration of metal was found in area KK, just south of the largest Apartment, III, and possibly associated kitchen Apartment II (see map of metal distribution), and also in that portion of area AA directly north of the north transept of the church. In other words, the district outside of the church, the Spanish Apartments I through VII and the cluster X through XIII, which we think well may have been the convent, apparently was the scene of most activity in casting away metal fragments and other Spanish imports and hence, we would deduce, the major scene of their storage, handling, and use.

Because so much more in metal fragments was found in what remained of room ZZ than in any other single room, it was suggested that the Spaniards could have used this room to serve as a blacksmithing center. One of the chunks of metal found there in room ZZ appeared to have been melted and solidified in an amorphous shape and some rod-like pieces of iron came from the same room. We know that metal rods were brought by the colonists to be used in repairs or made into needed articles. But if blacksmithing was associated with room ZZ, close to the center of the big house block, the work must have been done on an open second story space or in a room with roof removed so that sufficient light as well as opportunity for escape of smoke would have been provided.

Some melted metal also was found in area KK, on the south plaza directly south of room K, and it is possible that blacksmithing also was done out of doors here near the domed ovens at the southern corner of the East Plaza.

Kitchen equipment is noted once and again in the lists of what Oñate's men, especially those with families, were bringing with them (Hammond and Rey 1953:239,248), and these items can be checked against our multitude of metal fragments as offering some hint of possible identification for a few. *Comales* of iron, flat griddles on which tortillas and other comestibles could be cooked, would have been of relatively thin sheet metal, probably up to 1/8 inch thick before corrosion set in. The *comal* brought by some of the settlers was described as of copper, less weighty than those of iron and hence easier to handle as well as to pack, and it is quite possible that some of our scraps of sheet copper had been parts of such griddles. Of the heavy iron kettles noted in the same lists, we found two groups of fragments, plus one entire iron pot, fortunately not badly corroded. In this, meat would have been boiled, alone or as stew into which anything else available at the time probably would have been added. Such pots would have been heavy but infinitely easier to use without breakage than the jars of micaceous ware obtained from local Pueblo potters.

And iron otherwise? Oñate's list (Hammond and Rey 1953:216) includes 4,890 horseshoes for horses, mules and burros. We found several still recognizable. To go with his horseshoes, he included 79,000 nails. As for other nails, 13,000 "short nails" (Hammond and Rey 1953:216) were recorded, their actual length not given. Of those we recovered, except for the railroad spikes which clearly had come from the early Denver and Rio Grande Railroad of which the old station's foundation lay only a few feet from the ends of our east exploratory trenches, we could not judge the original length of the artifacts because of their bent, corroded, and often broken condition. We would suggest that they had been, probably, between 5 and 6 inches long.

Plowshares, adzes, small saws, chisels, axes of two sizes, augers, and padlocks are mentioned in the inventory lists; except for one axe, we recognized none in our fragments and neither did Dr. Arthur Woodward who kindly sorted over the whole. Scissors? Yes, out of the 89 pairs of "ordinary scissors" listed, we retrieved one half of a single pair.

We have already mentioned finding armor, iron chain armor to protect the upper torso and brass chain armor with smaller links to fall over the neck for decorative protection. We also found a wristlet, but whatever other pieces from such equipment may have remained had to go into our category of fragments because we could not recognize them. One could hardly picture any more uncomfortable outer covering, whether in the hot sun of summer or the chilling cold of winter, and our guess is that it was worn rather rarely. There also was horse armor, probably equally uncomfortable and now equally unrecognizable.

One copper spoon is listed on Oñate's inventory. The one we found had a hand-fashioned bowl and may never have had a handle, like the old pewter medicine spoons of our ancestors. Among our odds and ends is a metal knife ferule, the ring-like band which fastened knife blade to handle. Buckles? One of copper, identified by Woodward as probably having been made in Mexico as part of the fastening of a traveling trunk or, perhaps, as the buckle by which a man hung his sword from his body.

The King had paid for three bronze field pieces. Two others, apparently smaller also were listed, plus "an iron culvarin." To which of these the considerably corroded "iron canon ball" we found in area KK near Apartment II and III and the two domed oven bases we can not say. Storage for the field pieces we would guess had been in one of the nearby first floor rooms.

Our pair of what we called "cups for weighing," small copper vessels an inch or less in diameter (two sizes which fit into each other), came from a room of the West Mound group. Into one of these the hopeful miner would place his bit of gold dust or other treasure to be weighed on a balance scale, even as still is done in some assay offices. Handfuls of assorted mineral specimens evidently were being brought in from the countryside by men whose thoughts were not primarily on farming; we found such samples widely strewn through San Gabriel.

## Categories Intended for Trade

A hawk bell? The small bronze hawk bells of old Spain, there attached to the leg of a hawk or related bird in the practice of falconry, were very similar to the old sleigh bells of the eastern United States. American Indians of the historic period loved them and their descendants love them still, not for hawking but as a part of a dance costume. Oñate (Hammond and Rey 1953:221) had included 19 1/2 dozen hawk bells in his list of goods for trade. Had the Spaniard who left the lone sample we found in a West Mound room filched one from the general store with the thought of seeing what it would bring in trade? Or was he by chance an aficionado with hawks or trying to become so while in the lonely and unappreciated wilds of the Rio Grande Valley?

One of the most intriguing of the metal finds was a thin copper finger ring found in 1960, its rear portion now missing but apparently of a size to fit a fourth or fifth finger of a small to medium sized person. A raised approximately rectangular "set" of the same copper decorated the center front and a simple raised design of something approaching four overlapping partial circles flanked it on each side. Unfortunately, when recognized and picked up, it was lying on top of the hard packed back dirt which had been taken out of room 29, near the center of the west mound, presumably the summer before.

Another heading in the inventory of Oñate's goods covered nineteen "small Flemish mirrors," of which we found remains (our noses close to the soil), two minute bits appeared in the bottom of one of the East Plaza trenches. Or perhaps the mirrors from which our fragments were broken had been begged or appropriated by some of the women of the camp, even if originally listed under "articles of barter."

Of those goods for barter, the largest collection of all was made up of beads: 141,400 small glass beads of several colors, blue dominating, 63 rosaries of glass beads and some wooden beads ("painted like coral") for 7 more rosaries, 63 necklaces of glass beads, 44 throat bands of glass beads, 7 small bunches of little white beads, and "some beads of an alloy for throatbands," all in the inventory. In our last season, we found 7 glass beads, blue dominating, the majority from our Spanish layer in our East Plaza trenches.

## THE BIRTH AND DEATH OF OÑATE'S CITY OF SAN GABRIEL AS RECONSTRUCTED BY AN ANTHROPOLOGIST

The primary differences we could distinguish between the West Mound group of rooms and the Main Spanish Section, the big house block running northward into the "East Mound" as occupied in the Spanish Colonial Period, now can be briefly stated.

As far as we could determine, the West Mound either had no "Apartments" or all most none of the type made by cutting floor level doorways between rooms or out into a plaza. We must remember, however, that in what we dug we were not seeing the exterior rooms which originally had bordered on the adjoining plazas. Those outer rooms had been cut and bulldozed away long before we ever saw the site. If this house block was taken over as barracks, however, it is quite possible that no such efforts ever were made by or for the single men therein quartered. Apartments definitely had been arranged in reworking the Main Spanish House Block for use of Oñate, his captains, the convent for the friars, and possibly others. This could be recognized even for the first story at the south, southwest, and southeast peripheries of that block. It is possible, of course, that connecting doorways between rooms on the second floor may have provided Apartments in all three areas without any evidence of those modifications now being visible in the remaining walls of the bottom story. Access to second story living quarters, whether rooms or apartments, would have been by outside or inside ladders leading to "landing stages," roofs of first story rooms from which the second story rooms were set back several feet.

The presence of the church at what evidently was the south central or southeastern edge of the main plaza was according to Spanish town layouts of the day, and one would expect that the churchmen and the men of primary secular-political importance in this venture would have resided near each other. We have described Apartment XIII, which we believe to have been the monastery complete with kitchen, only a few feet distant from the north side of the church. Apartment III, with its three large rooms and quite possibly an association with next door Apartment II, which had a kitchen, always has appealed to us as appropriate for Oñate's headquarters, but the only conceivable evidence which has appeared is the presence of imported glassware and numerous sherds of Majolica table ware in Apartment III as well as in Apartment II.

# The Birthing of San Gabriel: the Little Things That Define a Lifestyle

Reading the pages of detailed lists covering what Oñate and some of his captains and their families were bringing into New Mexico may produce something of a sense of fairy tale rather than of historic reality. The colonists had enlisted with the understanding that they were moving into New Mexico on a permanent basis, not simply exploring or visiting. Such intent had been emphasized in the planning both to those who would serve in the stratified rank of leaders and to the "soldier-colonists" as such.

But for Oñate to include two state coaches and yards of Chinese and other taffeta and damask of several colors (Hammond and Rey 1953:226,219) reminds one that when he left Mexico he expected to establish a "city," size unstated but obviously not a hamlet. He and his officers, as officials, certainly never were to be farmers. Society would remain stratified, Spanish style, and the people present would live according to the customs of those social strata. When Oñate could not gain the cooperation of his colonists in the considerable labor of constructing a community, he struck from another angle and saw to it that the modifications he could order made in the old pueblo, Yungue, which he commandeered, would produce a Spanish town overall, if not in detail.

The reconstruction and repair were indeed widespread, as the details of our excavations proved. Some broken-down or otherwise undesirable structures apparently were removed except for a few sections of old walls which could be covered. The majority were stabilized where needed and, at least in the Main Spanish Area pierced with floor level doorways to create apartments of up to three plaza level rooms. The foundations of a few rooms were improved, some or all walls were given a new coat of adobe plaster, and firepits were put into the new adobe-covered floors. These firepits, as constructed for or by the Spaniards, were literally nothing more than holes, pits, neither neatly clay-plastered nor slab-lined as the Pueblo people had meticulously finished theirs for hundreds of years. We can be sure the Pueblo people were properly shocked at the Spaniards' lack of interest in the possible niceties of household fireboxes.

In contrast, the Spaniards understood the use of raised fire hearth cookery, the hearth a basal construction of cobbles on which a fire of wood or charcoal would be built a few inches off the floor. The smoke could be handled via an old European style hood which reached out from the wall above the hearth to provide a draft through one or more European style roof chimneys. A simpler solution would have been trusting that the hot smoke, like that from the Pueblo firepit, would naturally rise to escape through the hatchway which also provided an opening for the ladder leading from the first story floor up to the second. As far as we found, however, such cooking arrangements were present in only two apartments, by which we would conclude that they could only have been for the most elite.

The entire job of reconstruction and repair obviously was accomplished rapidly, between, at the latest, midwinter of 1600 when Oñate's second contingent arrived from Mexico, and the summer of 1601 when Oñate took a party out onto the Plains and the dissidents left in camp met in the new church and decided to desert. The Pueblo women, who needed the pay offered in food and who customarily did all but the heavier parts of construction of their own homes, probably did the major portion of labor on houses to be occupied by the Spaniards, but the church of San Miguel, which must have been put up at the same time, was of stone and probably built by Indian men directed by the friars.

Some of the foodstuffs dispersed in pay may have come from the agricultural efforts reported as made by at least a part of the Spanish population, but it also is possible that a portion of the food commandeered by the Spaniards from the scanty stores of the Indians may have been paid back to them as the price of labor. There is no question that the very real and drastic two season drought of 1600-1601 (Smiley, Stubbs, and Bannister 1953) was an unexpected and very forceful factor in the twisted history of Oñate's colony and his dream.

No mention of tableware (plates, cups, platters, bowls, large or small) is to be found in the list of goods packed for transportation to New Mexico, but in 1597 Oñate presented 43 carts, of which 24 were his own and 19 belonged to his lieutenant, captains, and soldiers. He also had 3 others with iron rimmed wheels, to be drawn by mules, and the friars had "six equipped carts, with six mules for each" (Hammond and Rey 1953:138). A part of the household equipment evidently deemed necessary to the homes envisioned for the leaders was crockery and glass. Whether the dishes were set upon low benches substituted for tables or simply on a piece of tanned skin laid on the floor (as in later centuries) we do not know.

The standard tableware of the Spaniards of upper class in Mexico during the sixteenth century apparently was Majolica (maiolica) ware, at first fairly scarce but becoming more common as the century wore on and economic conditions improved (Lister and Lister 1982). Some was imported from Spain, but most used in America seems to have been produced by small potterias in Puebla, Mexico, and in or near Mexico City itself as early as 1540. In both these centers it continued to be made during the seventeenth and eighteenth centuries, with variations in named types, associated shapes, and styles of design. Modern variants of this hand-made ware still are offered for sale in Mexico today.

It is not surprising, then, that among the many native potsherds (23 Rio Grande Pueblo pottery types represented in the fill still remaining in rooms or redeposited in the area of our east trenches at San Gabriel), we found a thin scattering (23 examples) of blue-on-white Majolica, green-on-white, yellow, green, and brown-on-white, and even a touch of reddish orange-on-white. The paste for this ware commonly was more or less of an apricot hue. In San Gabriel, as in Mexico, the Majolica was associated with Chinese porcelain (3 examples) in blue on white and orange on white, the designs and finish delicate and precise and the thickness of sherds but a fraction of that of the Majolica ware. The porcelain was being brought in to Mexico by the sixteenth-seventeenth century flourishing China trade.

It was from the forms in Majolica ware of this period that our Rio Grande Pueblo potters began copying the shape we refer to as "the Spanish soup plate," whether in actual soup plate or sauce dish size bowls, and it also was through copying the low raised band which encircles many Majolica bowl bases that some of the sixteenth-seventeenth century potters of New Mexico borrowed the concept of placing the foreign-looking ring base on a very few of their own bowls and jars.

Certain of the Pueblo potters evidently found sale for or were ordered to produce for Yungue's leading families a few large "coffee cups," flat bottomed, with straight but low sides, and with the vertical handle still familiar to us. The surface of the two we found had never been covered with the native glaze (lead, a bit of copper, and flux) but only decorated with designs of the heavy contemporary Rio Grande type with which several Pueblo groups were adept in the 1600s.

Why did Oñate's dream for San Gabriel end in failure and, for some years, his personal disgrace?

As one puts the archaeological evidence together with the bits to be abstracted from documents pertaining to the Oñate expedition and establishment of San Gabriel, it becomes evident that the majority of those persons we are customarily admonished to think of as "soldier colonists" were primarily soldier-adventurers, not really colonists by intent.

Certainly but few actually were colonists in the sense that the primary concern of such a group might be predicted as settlement of land in the name of their country, and actual subjugation of that land in establishing a dependable source of food and other personal and group necessities. By the second year of the drought, 1601, the Indians, now without any reserve stores of their own because the Spaniards had forced them to give up what little they had, were subsisting by parching wild seeds and dry plant stems with embers in hot sand (not eating corn stalks and trash from the fields mixed with charcoal, as described by the non-too observant outsiders). The historical papers (testimony from Fray Lopez Izquierdo, guardian of the convent, is a good example) reiterate the forceful acquisition of even very small amounts of hidden corn, though it required torture of the natives, "lest the army perish" (Hammond and Rey 1953:676-681).

In 1601 the Spaniards themselves were reported to be killing seven cattle each week and so, only three years after their arrival, had none left from those brought by the original colonists but only those animals Oñate's supplementary group had driven up from Mexico (Hammond and Rey 1953:651). One might expect that our next paragraph would cover some data relating to the number of animals being killed by "colonists" in the nearby mountains, or of fish taken from the river, as energetically pursued supplements to San Gabriel's rapidly disappearing food supply.

Not so. During our three seasons of excavations, we retrieved approximately 500 No. 10 paper bags full of animal bones from the rooms, outside "areas," East Plaza, and especially, the East Plaza trenches of San Gabriel. These trenches, already described, were into the area which had served the Spaniards as their major location for trash deposition and, together with area KK near the ovens, provided a large proportion of our bone specimens. These, turned over to Dr. Arthur H. Harris at the Museum of Arid Land Biology of the University of Texas in El Paso for study, provide the only data existent covering what animals had been utilized by the people of San Gabriel and in what relative proportions.

In his report (Harris 1969) we learn that close to two thirds of our recovered faunal remains represented domestic species, including "all mammals usually utilized today for work, food, or pets except the domestic cat."

Horse and burro bones were present in small numbers. Those of the horse indicate that animals of medium to slightly less than medium size had been brought out of Mexico but for some reason eventually had died. The same was true for the burros, which physically were very much like those of today.

Approximately one fourth of the bones collected were those of domestic cattle, quite variable in size. What little evidence was available suggested that their type was somewhat more similar to that of the longhorn we know for the American period in the Southwest than like that of our modern cattle with rather evenly curved horns.

The records indicate that both sheep and goats were among the animals driven to the colony. Although the bones of the two are difficult to separate, it seems that sheep were considerably more numerous than goats. We all know that lamb and "cabrito" (young goat) are more tasty than mutton or grown goats, but in circumstances where the most meat producible would

80

seem to be a point in choosing the age for slaughter of a definitely limited number of animals, our colonists were butchering the majority before the close of their second year when they would have attained their full growth.

Bon apetit.*

As for domestic pigs, their remains are not as numerous as those of the larger animals, for it seems that a great many were killed while young and very few left to grow into full adults and hence to reproduce once and again. Roast suckling pig still is a great favorite in the best restaurants of Madrid, and domed oven roasting would have been practical.

Very nice if one can afford the rapid disappearance of limited domestic livestock.

As for the category of domesticated pets rather than animals required for use or food, we had remains from two dogs of different sizes. We did not come across any statement as to whether the Spaniards brought such animals with them (it seems likely), but we do know that when the ancestors of the North American Indians crossed the Bering Straits from Asia, they were accompanied by dogs. Our find of several dog tracks ranging from distinct to indistinct proved that three hundred and fifty years earlier at least one dog had run back and forth over what that day was muddy ground but eventually would be marked with yellow cord to indicate the west end limit for excavation in Trench 14.

And the wild animals we postulated as a supplement to the disappearing food supply?

In those 55 bags of animal bones there was evidence of only 45 mule deer, 4 prong horn antelope, and 4 bighorn sheep. The only other animals represented in any number were cottontails and jackrabbits, with a very few pocket gophers and prairie dogs. And of course we cannot be certain that all the bones we found had belonged to animals taken by the Spaniards rather than by the Indians, especially when we remind ourselves that our potsherds covering three centuries in types were found thoroughly mixed together.

Evidently the soldier colonists were not sportsmen or Oñate feared to have them out in small parties in the mountain area.

It was at this point in Oñate's multitudinous problems that he decided he finally had enough men, including his supplementary group recently out of Mexico, so that it should be safe to divide them and take a small party

---

\*     Almost total lack of charred bones makes it fairly certain that meat certainly was neither being spit-barbecued nor roasted except, perhaps, within the domed ovens. Stewing would have been the most common technique of preparation.

out onto the Plains to the east. He had two objects in mind: discovering whether any wealth or food sources might possibly be available there, either obviously being a source of improved PR in San Gabriel if found, and, at the same time, intending to learn whether buffalo, adults or calves, could be brought back to camp and domesticated.

His experiment, unfortunately, yielded no profitable solutions to Spanish problems. By the time his party returned to San Gabriel, his fate and that of his colony had been sealed by the deserters. That included all but one of the Franciscans, who commissioned those deserters to deliver a personal letter to his superiors in Mexico stating his own feeling that someone must remain with the new church, though his sympathy was with the group abandoning the camp.

We would describe this action of desertion as resulting from the general wave of self sympathy, boredom, a near-panic fear of real famine and starvation, and a general desire to blame the overall feeling of non-success on of course the Governor. There long had been some stress between the religious group and Oñate, the former feeling that the leader's punishments of disobedient young Spaniards and similarly of rebellious Indians were too violent and led to increased stress as well as to native refusals of religious conversion.

Fray Francisco de Zamora's statement, representing the churchmen, appears to have been a realistic testament to matters as the friars saw them:

> ... they [the natives] did not show as great an inclination toward teaching as we should have liked in order to encourage us to redouble our efforts to teach them, and, ... because all of the people who came here with us and those who have come since have done gross injury to the natives of the land in order to keep alive. They took away from them by force all the food that they had gathered for many years, without leaving them any for the support of themselves and their children, robbed them of the scanty clothing they had to protect themselves, their women and children, causing the natives much harm and wounding their feelings. This brought great discredit to our teaching for they said that if we who are Christians caused so much harm and violence, why should they become Christians.
>
> (Hammond and Rey 1953:675)

One needs to add only that the Pueblo people, even to the present, keep their languages untaught to outsiders as far as possible, so that they can discuss matters between themselves without revealing their reactions to persons not a part of their own group. Further, the Pueblo people to whom conservatism is one of their most important values, for a great many generations had based their agriculture and their lives on "the old religion." Eventually, yes, they would accept Christianity, but not without time to think and understand and finally see their way to combining the new faith with that which had been the mainstay of their ancestors throughout the long centuries of survival in a difficult environment. It is thus today.

Oñate, in contrast to the friars, believed that his measures were necessary in securing, as far as possible, fairness to the natives and security for his colony, a small unit in a new land with relatively massive and widespread population, even if the natives were on their own feet and armed only with bows and arrows in contrast to the lesser Spanish population equipped with guns and horses.

So the friars and the laymen, the later probably having been, in the main, adventurers hoping for something good to turn up while they dutifully served the king, took their rapid and surreptitious departure in some cases stealing away with the trunks and boxes of goods left in their care by the loyal few then out on the Plains with Oñate. Oñate, his fortune expended, would be returned to Mexico and prison but eventually pardoned. Don Pedro de Peralta would lead the colonists who still wanted to live in New Mexico on the new venture of settling Santa Fe. The old site was returned to the Indians, but although they took over the farmlands, until the 1900s the Pueblos, mistrusting the obvious insecurity of walls pierced by window openings and surface level doors, merely buried their dead in the old mounds but did not move back into San Gabriel del Yungue.

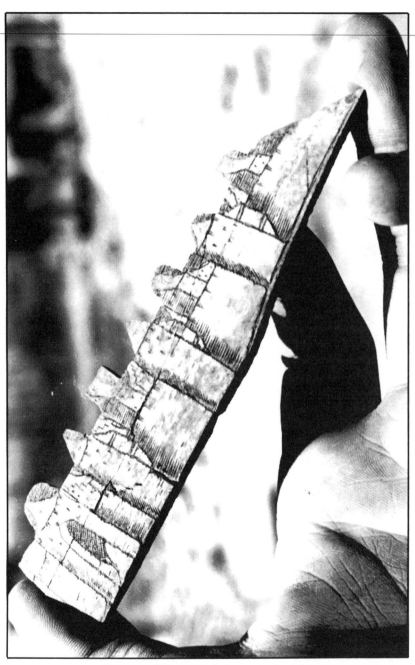

*Engraved Gunstock inset in hand*

# P. S.

There are moments when the world seems to draw together in space and time, and a man as a human being struggling with the personal problems to which he finds himself heir emerges as a symbol of us all.

The topmost of all our exciting finds was an arquebus stock inlay, hand incised, probably by a young volunteer from Flanders in a scene as old as the Pueblo adobe walls against which he rested his back while he carved. One of those everyday persons, like the rest of us, a colonist who had dutifully signed to make the long trek up the Rio Grande into unknown lands for reasons which were not his own but stemming from the tangled strands of world history.

It was midday and midsummer in 1962, and hot, much like the day when we first found the morning glory patch and the remains of the Spanish Apartments beneath the flowers. Lee Montoya, employed to help us break through the rough water-hardened surface crust overlying the top of our east mound trenches, brought down his pick with vigor, noted that he had cracked a bone lying on or just beneath that surface, and picked up the artifact.

Ivory inlays for fine gunstocks and even for the stocks of crossbows are known for European weapons of the late sixteenth-seventeenth centuries, but this bone inlay, as it was recognized to be, contrasted with the European specimens both in material and in simplicity of workmanship. The scene, immediately recognizable when the piece was washed, depicted a walled-European city of the Middle Ages, its high curved wall turreted at intervals, a great arched gateway giving entrance through that heavy wall, and the tall terraced gable roofs of city houses projecting above wall, towers, and turrets. In New Mexico? Yes, on the outskirts of a site of the same age but halfway across a world ever beset with the problems man creates for himself.

We were close to the end of our last season at San Gabriel, and State Governor Ed Mechem, James T. Forrest, Director of the Museum of New Mexico, Bruce T. Ellis, Historian for the Museum, and Stewart Peckham Archaeologist from the Laboratory of Anthropology already had been out to enthusiastically inspect what remained of rooms and goods from the first capital of New Mexico. One of the most famous of Spain's newswriters, Guy Bueno, who had been at the Spanish embassy in Washington when the news of our finds broke in Time Magazine , an article written by the then newspaperman Tony Hillerman, and a dozen newspapers spread through the United States also had flown out to pick up a new wisp of history involving the people of Spain.

It was a young friend, a former student, Annette Ewing, at this time working for an advanced degree in History and fortunately chancing to have some background in European art and architecture of our period, who first put us on the track of the towns which might have been depicted in our carving, as well as probable identification of the carver.

In the sixteenth century walled cities had been common all through Europe. Some of their walls were crenelated but had not been interrupted by towers and turrets nor, as ours showed, had high gabled houses with sharply terraced roofs behind them. The area most distinguished for the emphatic terracing of its high roofs was Flanders. Ambitious Spain, before and after the brief period of San Gabriel del Yungue, claimed control over much of Flanders, a portion of Belgium as we know it today. Quickly seeking the mutual aid possible between history and archaeology, Annette sent me a quotation from Hammond and Rey's roster of Oñate's enlistees for the great adventure (my own two volumes being safely at home in Santa Fe at the time):

> Rodrigo Velmán, son of Francisco Velmán, native of Trimonia, Flemish, of medium stature, red-bearded, 33 years of age, with his arms, which the governor [Oñate] had given him, he said.          (Hammond and Rey 1953:300)

Oñate's enlistees included only the one Flemishman.

But where was Trimonia?

This village either must have been small enough to have disappeared, or been overlooked in the day of modern maps, or, very possibly, had its name changed sometime in the past, like so many of the towns in that general area. But, nine years later, following our little lead by foot and by car, I made a careful inspection of what still remained of the old city wall of Brussels, one of the Belgian cities which has cherished its past. That wall very much resembled - but did not quite duplicate - the wall shown on our inlay. Unfortunately, the ancient houses once close behind it had been torn down: nothing now remained but foundations. Across the narrow old street, however, many examples of that type of house still stood (1971), the majority with sharply gabled and terraced ends outlining steep roofs. In the big central plaza of the guild houses, in little plazas with fountains, and up the hill near the old church and cathedral, the houses lining the edge of the cobbled streets were of this type. In Spain and in Germany we found other excellent examples of city walls interrupted by towers but without the turrets depicted on our inlay. Several of the old walls still existent are crenelated, like that of the bone inlay, but others, though similarly pierced with slits through which archers could sight and shoot, had a smooth top edge, as still to be seen at Rothenburg, Germany, and Carcasonne in southern France. The old walls of Seville, like that of Olité, Spain, were crenelated but the houses inside them were not of the terraced gable type.

Flanders was known as the center of this architectural style depending heavily on the terraced or stepped high gable roof, sometimes simply handled and sometimes elaborated by added motifs. Peter Brugel, the Elder (1530-1569) and his son, Peter the Younger (1564-1638), show such houses once and again in their lively paintings of Flemish village life and festivities, as exhibited in various European museums and art publications.

What, then, can we conclude? Our best guess is that Rodrigo Velmán, unmarried adventurer, leaned back against a sun-warmed adobe wall and eased a longing for home and something he could better comprehend than the colonization of New Mexico for the good of Spain and the saving of native souls through their semi-understood but immediately required acceptance of Catholicism. He had no ivory, but he had a choice of bones from those animals painfully herded up from Mexico and consumed with such rapidity. According to the Spaniards, their animals disappeared the sooner in that many died because of poor pasturage. According to the Indians, the Spaniards let their animals into the Pueblo fields to graze, which understandably, brought the crops of those fields to a speedy end.

We cannot prove that Velmán incised the gunstock decoration, but it seems most likely. We cannot prove that he was remembering in correct detail any specific city wall and the houses behind it; it seems more likely that he was portraying a generalized Medieval city as seen from outside the wall, but from a Flemish viewpoint. Did he ever set the decoration into his gunstock? Probably not, for if he had, the whole would have gone back to Mexico intact.

We do not know even where he left his little piece of art work, for it is quite certain that it landed on the surface of our east trench area via some of the bulldozing work done years earlier by Mr. Montoya himself.

--------------------

Our new picture of existence in Spanish-occupation of San Gabriel del Yungue includes living quarters primarily on a second story, with the ground level story utilized principally for what considerable storage was necessary and, in the convent (Apartment XIII) and also in Apartment II to the east, for specialized kitchens. Our finds of 23 fragments of imported glassware and of 18 of Majolica ware (almost all from the main house mound and east plaza of San Gabriel) spells out a standard of living in this concentrated area near the church above that of the "soldier colonists," as such. We are most fortunate in finally having the half-outline of the per-

~~manent church of San Miguel, and to also have its old candleholders. We~~
even have that bit of lacy gold braid "galloon" which once decorated the
vestment of a friar who presided here, as well as chunks (and individual
links) of rusted chain mail which provided gunmen with at least psychologi-
cal confidence against those who still fought with bows and arrows.

Apart from the details learned when artifacts are found and architecture
uncovered, one lesson herein is - unhappily - emphasized. This site, of
major importance historically and its location generally though not specifi-
cally known for 300 years, should and could have been spotted and
protected long before it received that limited but all important touch of interested recognition in the 1940s. Who, except for Bandelier, ever had
bothered himself to ask the people of San Juan Pueblo where Yungue had
stood, where the first Spanish colonists had lived. The natives knew the
general location from tradition, even if they could not point a finger to the
specific site of the old church. When we asked, they told us it had stood at
the southern edge of the main plaza of Yungue, which is precisely where
we found it. How did it happen that except for a single advisory and friend-
ly warning from the Indian Service after the general location of San Gabriel
was determined by Marjorie Tichy (Lambert), no one did anything about
persuading the Indians to desist from building on top of the remnants of the
mounds, - "remnants" because the tops and sides of those mounds already
had been bulldozed and much of the architectural material and cultural artifacts removed without ever having been seen even by the bulldozer
operators? Then came the long years of irrigation of crops planted on top
of what remained of the foundations and wall stubs. After that, there were
our three seasons of archaeological work, at the invitation of the Pueblo but
ever hurried because we had been warned that some of the villagers were
not comfortable with the concept of excavation and that others wanted to
spread their own occupation even farther over the present surface.

In August of 1962 we soaked our excavated rooms with kerosene, recovered the floors with soil, and paid some of the San Juan men to lay new
adobe bricks along the tops of the old walls, all for protection, and to fill-
in overall with more soil for preservation.

Today, once more, much of the old site is again under cultivation.

What is there left to do? Test pits to discover precisely how far the site
originally extended. Excavation where possible - and if at all practical, with
complete sifting in order to retrieve every possible artifact, no mater how
small. We, ourselves, never dared take the time for total sifting; we sifted
where there appeared to be reason.

In its first stage, Yungue was a long-lasting and successful pueblo. In its
second stage, as San Gabriel del Yungue, it was in large part not
reconstructed but revised to alleviate some of the Spaniards' discomfort at

living under conditions to which they and their ancestors had not been accustomed. San Gabriel was the second Spanish settlement in what is now the United States. Here we have a different story from that of San Marcos and we also have much more of the physical remnants than were preserved in Florida. What is left should be saved, a symbol of cultural heritage for three peoples: Pueblo, Spanish, and Anglo.

# Bibliography

Anderson, A.J.O., and C.E. Dibble 1950 General History of the Things of New Spain. Fray Bernadino de Sahagun. Florentine Codex, Book I, The Gods. Monographs of the School of American Research, No. 14, Pt. II. Santa Fe.

Adams, Eleanor B. and Fray Angelico Chavez 1956 The Missions of New Mexico, 1776, Description by Fray Atonasio Dominguez.Translation and Annotation. UNM Press. Albuquerque.

Bandelier, Adolph F.A. 1890 Final Report of Investigation Among the Indians of the Southwestern United States, Carried on Mainly in the Years from 1880 to 1885. Vol. I. Papers of the Archaeological Institute of America, American Series 3. Cambridge, Mass.

Bandelier, Adolph F.A. 1892 Final Report of Investigation Among the Indians of the Southwestern United States, Carried on Mainly in the Years from 1880 to 1885. Vol. II. Papers of the Archaeological Institute of America American Series 4. Cambridge, Mass.

Bolton, Herbert E. 1930 Spanish Expeditions in the Southwest. New York.

Boyd, E. 1943 Antiques in New Mexico. Antiques, Vol. XVIV:2:58-62. New York.

Boyd, E. 1961 Bronze Medal of Sixteenth Century Style. El Palacio 68:2:124-128.

Breternitz, David A. 1966 An Appraisal of Tree-Ring Dated Pottery in the Southwest.. Anthropological Papers of the University of Arizona 10. Tucson.

Caso, Alfonso and Michael D. Coe 1958 The Aztecs. People of the Sun.,Norman, Ed. G. Daniel. New York.

Dozier, Edward P. 1970 The Pueblo Indians of North America Case Studies in Cultural Anthropology Eds. G. and L. Spindler, Standford.

Ellis, Florence Hawley    1964 Archaeological History of Nambé Pueblo, Fourteenth Century to the Present. American Antiquity 30:34-42.

—    1970 Irrigation and Water Works in the Rio Grande. Ms. Paper given at the Pecos Conference Symposium Santa Fe, New Mexico.

—    1970 San Gabriel del Yunque: Window on the PreSpanish Indian World. Ms. 20 pgs.

—    1987 The Long Lost "City" of San Gabriel Del Yungue, Second Oldest European Settlement in the United States. When Cultures Meet, Remembering San Gabriel del Yunge Oweenge. (sic) Sunstone Press, Santa Fe.

—    1989 Yungue. Paper given at New Mexico Archaeological Council Nov 1988, and to be subsequently published by them.

Fontana, Bernard L.    1987 San Gabriel del Yungue Oweenge, (sic) Southwestern Mission Research Center Newsletter Vol. 21:70:5-6 Aug. 1987.

Forrest, Earl R.    1929 Missions and Pueblos of the Old Southwest, Their Myths, Legends, Fiestas, and Ceremonies, with some accounts of the Indian Tribes and their Dances and of the Penitentes, Arthur H. Clark Co. Cleveland, U.S.A. (Reprinted by Rio Grande Press), Chicago, 1965.

Fink, Colin G. and E. P. Polushkin    1946 Metalographic Examination of the San Gabriel Bell Fragment. New Mexico Historical Review XXI:2:145-148. Santa Fe.

Harris, Arthur H.    1969 The Mammalion Remains from Yungue Ms. 39 pgs. Museum of Arid Land Biology. The University of Texas at El Paso.

Hammond, George P. and Agapito Rey    1940 Narratives of the Coronado Expedition. UNM Press. Albuquerque.

Hammond, George P. and Agapito Rey    1953 Don Juan de Oñate: Colonizer of New Mexico, 1595-1628. Coronado Quarto Centennial Publication, Vol. I and II. UNM Press. Albuquerque.

Hawley, Florence          1931 Chemistry in Prehistoric American Arts. Journal of Chemical Education 8:3542.

Hawley, Florence, and      1938 Classification of Black Pottery Pigments
    Fred G. Hawley         and paint areas. University of New Mexico Bulletin, Anthropological Series 2:4 :314.

Hawley, Florence, and      1946 Group Designed Behavior Patterns in
    Donovan Senter         Two Acculturating Groups. Southwestern Journal of Anthropology, Vol. 2:2:133-151. Albuquerque.

Hodge, Frederick W.       1907 Castañeda: Narrative of the Expedition of Coronado. Spanish Explorers in the Southern United States, 1528-1543. New York.

Hodge, Fredrick Web,      1945 Fray Alonso de Benavides Revised
    George P. Hammond and     Memorial of 1634. UNM Press.
    Agipito Rey            Albuquerque.

Jeancon, J.A.            1923 Excavations in the Chama Valley, New Mexico. Bureau of American Ethnology Bulletin 31. Washington.

Jimenez Moreno,          1966 MesoAmerica Before the Toltecs.
    Wigberto             Ancient Oaxaca Ed. John Paddock. Stanford.

Johnson, Chester        1961 A Note on the Excavation of Yungue, San Gabriel. El Palacio 68:2:121-124.

Lambert, Marjorie F.     1952 Oldest Armor in the U.S. Discovered at San Gabriel del Yungue. El Palacio 59:3:83-87. (Description of the find by José Abeyta and note of Marge's work also on find of "piece of bronze bell" by Stephen Trujillo.)

—                      1953 The Oldest Armor found in the United States. The San Gabriel del Yunque Helmet. Archaeology 6:2:108-110.

—                      1954 A Recently Discovered Sword of the Late Seventeenth or Early Eighteenth Century. El Palacio 61:9:300-305.

Mera, Harry P.          1935 Ceramic Clues to the Prehistory of North Central New Mexico. New Mexico Archaeological Survey, Laboratory of Anthropology Technical Series Bulletin 8. Santa Fe.

| | | |
|---|---|---|
| Nordenskiold, G. | 1893 | The Cliff Dwellers of Mesa Verde: their pottery and Implements Chicago. |
| Ortiz, Alfonso | 1969 | The Tewa World. Chicago. |
| Parsons, Elsie Clewes | 1929 | The Social Organization of the Tewa of New Mexico. American Anthropological Association, Memoirs No. 36. Menasha. |
| Parsons, Elsie Clewes | 1939 | Pueblo Indian Religion, Vol. I, II. Chicago. |
| Peterson, Harold L. | 1952 | The Helmet Found at San Gabriel del Yungue, New Mexico. El Palacio 59:9:283-287 (Identification plus data on methods used for its preservation by Peterson.) |
| Scholes, France V. | 1937 | Church and State in New Mexico, 1610-1650. Historical Society of New Mexico Publications in History, Vol. VII. Albuquerque. |
| Schroeder, Albert H. | 1968 | Shifting for Survival. New Mexico Historical Review XLIII:4:291-310 |
| Smiley, Terah L., Stanley A. Stubbs, and Byrant Bannister | 1953 | A Foundation for the Dating of Some Late Archaeological Sites in the Rio Grande Area, New Mexico: Based on Studies in Tree-Ring Methods and Pottery Analysis. Laboratory of Tree-Ring Research Bulletin No. 6. University of Arizona Bulletin. Tucson. |
| Stowe, Noel R. | 1982 | A Preliminary Report on the Pine Log Creek Site Ba 462. Ms. University of South Alabama Archaeological Research Laboratory. Mobile, Alabama. |
| Stubbs, Stanley A. W.S. Stallings, Jr. | 1953 | The Excavation of Pindi Pueblo, New Mexico. Monographs of the School of American Research No. 18, Santa Fe. |
| Tichy, Marjorie F. | 1944 | Exploratory Work at Yuque Yunque. El Palacio LI:11:222-224. |
| — | 1946 | New Mexico's First Capital. New Mexico Historical Review XXI:2: 140-144. (The "bell". Also data on Marge's excavation and recognition of it as site of Yunque Yunque, San Gabriel, in 1944. She had only one digger, a |

| | | |
|---|---|---|
| | | native. She quotes in this from the account of her brief work there.) |
| — | 1946 | First Capital Suffers Further Damage. El Palacio 53:11:324. |
| Villagrá, Gaspar Pérez de Acalá | 1933 | A History of New Mexico by Gaspar Pérez de Alcalá 1610. Translated from the Spanish by Gilbert Espenosa, Ed. Introduction and notes by F.W. Hodge. The Los Angeles Quivera Society, Vol. IV. Los Angeles. |
| Wendorf, Fred | 1953 | Salvage Archaeology in the Chama Valley, New Mexico. Monographs of the School of American Research, No. 17. Santa Fe. |

# INDEX